West Africa in History

VOLUME ONE

VOLUME TWO

SINCE 1800

A completely revised and expanded new edition

'Mr. Conton has not merely served up facts gleaned from the work of previous historians. He constantly requires his pupils to think and to discriminate.'

—Teacher Education

West Africa in History

BY W. F. CONTON

B.A.

Chief Education Officer, Sierra Leone
Sometime Headmaster, Accra High School, Ghana

VOLUME ONE

Before 1800

TO MY MOTHER

FIRST PUBLISHED IN 1961
SECOND IMPRESSION 1962
THIRD IMPRESSION 1963
FOURTH IMPRESSION 1964
FIFTH IMPRESSION 1965
REVISED NEW EDITION (SIXTH IMPRESSION) 1965

© William Conton

Second Edition © William Conton

INTRODUCTION

I first read my late father's history book a few years ago, at the grand old age of about sixty. I had been a stalwart science student, completely uninterested in history, and my father, God bless his soul, never tried to steer me or indeed any of his other children, in the direction of his field of study. When I finally did read the book I was impressed and felt that the book deserved to be kept alive. The concepts the author explores are still topical almost sixty years after the book was published. He is keen to demonstrate to his readers that Africa generally and West Africa in particular, have been equal partners in the development of mankind, that the then (and still) current position of Africa on the human development ladder is an aberration when viewed through the longer lens that history affords.

This book, the first of two volumes, takes the reader through 2,000 years of African history in less than 200 pages; it provides the general reader with a most interesting introduction to African history. Conceived as a school text for English-speaking West Africa and first published in 1961, it had been reprinted five times by 1965. But after independence, newly emergent nations wanted their own national histories, not regional ones. Nigeria wanted a history focusing on Nigeria; Ghana, on Ghana. School curricula changed, and the school market, far and away the biggest book market in African countries, shifted accordingly. And so the histories that covered an entire region, like this one, or continent even, fell out of favour and were superseded. Not only that; a history of Nigeria, for example, implies a history extending back only one or two hundred years to events surrounding the creation of what is a relatively recent entity. The new histories thus tended to be limited not only in space but also in time. In this earlier history, Conton has the freedom to range back thousands of years and to and fro across the vast West African landscape.

In his preface Conton sets forth the romantic vision of Africa that sustains him throughout the book, as he discusses the "shared memory of the greatness of ancient Ghana, Mali, Songhai, Bornu, Asante (Ashanti) and Benin". that "was temporarily lost…" and "…is now being regained."

As a non-historian I found the boldness of his presentation fascinating and very credibly researched: In Chapter 2 he unquestioningly quotes Herodotus, an ancient Greek scholar who claimed travelers circumnavigated Africa in classical times (ie the period from 400 B.C. to 400 A.D.) and described what these travelers found there; some scholars have questioned Herodotus' accuracy and veracity. Much later in the book the author describes the long, patient struggle of the Portuguese to traverse Africa and get to India. He is careful to detail many of the voyages, name the captains and describe the rivermouths and capes and mountains traversed, in an effort that lasted from 1419 until Vasco da Gama made India in 1495. If the Europeans had so much difficulty sailing round Africa, how, according to Herodotus, were the earlier travelers able to do this 2,000 years earlier? Conton offers no explanation but one suspects he might argue that the Egyptians self-evidently built the Sphinx and the great pyramids, and today's best minds are still not sure how they did it. He confidently broaches other controversial subjects; the possibility that at least some ancient Egyptians, perhaps even some of their kings, were black, the wealth and preeminence of early African kingdoms, the possibility that the Yoruba came from Egypt. In discussing the ancient kingdom of Ghana he affirms, *"Some history books may give you the impression that, because for brief periods of its history it fell under the rule of non-negro people, it was therefore not a true negro state. Such an impression would be false. Most of the people of the Empire were Soninkes, members of the very large Mande-speaking group of negro tribes."*and refers to the writings, starting from the eighth century, of Al-Fazari, Al-Bakri, Al-Masudi, Al-Gharnati, Idrisi and Ibn-Hawqal to back his position.

As a fellow writer I found the strength and consistency of his point of view, and the motivation for it, admirable; I admired the extent of his research, serving as the foundation for the firmness of his conclusions, particularly in the classical and pre-European eras, where the written record is more scanty. I admired all this even though, after 60 years of troubled African Independence, it's hard now to share his rosy assessment of the continent. All of which raises the question: *should* historians have a point of view? Shouldn't they just present us with the unadulterated facts? Partly through reading this book I've come to understand that in practice many, if not all, historians do have a point of view. Especially for events that occurred hundreds of years ago, there's no one certain, correct history. There are different histories, some well researched and laid out, some not. Conton was a relatively early proponent of what now has come to be known as the Afrocentric school of historians, engaged in a fierce debate with earlier, classical historians, who held that European development, with Greece at the epicenter, owed little or nothing to Africa. These classical historians came to the fore during the racism of the slave trade era and superseded earlier, ancient historians (such as Herodotus) who had outlined the contributions of Africa. Some Afrocentrists maintain that ancient Egypt, the most advanced civilization in the world at the time, originally was a black African nation, before being overrun by Arabs from the Arabian peninsula.

Conton uses all the armoury of the professional historian to justify his point of view: archaeological site investigations, surviving artifacts, African oral history and the written record of Greek, Roman, Persian, Arab and European historians.

Many contemporary questions arise in the reading of Conton's history. He was an uncritical admirer of the ancient African empires. As he describes repeatedly the greatness of Ghana, Mali, Songhai *et al* I found myself asking: What happened to all the wealth? What happened to all the gold that was mined and still is mined in so many parts of West Africa? Rather than marvel at the wealth of Mansa Musa (who we learn took 80 camels each bearing 300 lb. of gold on a pilgrimage to Mecca in 1324) and his fellow emperors, we would perhaps do better to use them as salutary lessons of profligate leadership from the past, perhaps reminiscent of profligate leadership of today! The empires covered vast swathes of West Africa, Conton tells us, illustrating vividly with maps. But should "greatness" be indicated at all by size, especially when this size is attained by the aggressive expansionism then common among the African empires? Is this then the way Africa needs to go? Aggregating larger and larger territories into a single state? Some might argue for the reverse.

Early in the book, Conton discusses Herodotus' description of a trip to the "Ethiopians", at the time apparently a formidable nation somewhere south of Egypt. Modern day historians are still struggling to learn about the ancient "Ethiopians" and to unravel the mysteries of Africa. Archaeological work still has much to reveal, as Conton was well aware. Just a few days ago (December, 2019), a new archaeological site, more than 2000 years old, from the ancient and formidable kingdom of Axum, in modern day Ethiopia, was announced to the world. Conton's confidence in Herodotus' controversial descriptions perhaps was justified after all!

Paul Conton
Freetown, December, 2019

P. 1 The Portuguese Invader in the eyes of an African Artist

TO PUPILS AND TEACHERS

History in West Africa since 1957 has been a cavalcade of independence. But, impressive and colourful as this movement has been, we shall not fully understand it unless we realize that behind the demand of the peoples of modern Nigeria, Ghana, Sierra Leone and the Gambia for their independence lies their shared memory of the greatness of ancient Ghana, Mali, Songhai, Bornu, Asante (Ashanti) and Benin. This memory is kept alive by our folk tales and songs, and by our splendid heritage of art.

So I have tried to recapture for you a little of that greatness, to show how it was temporarily lost, and how it is now being regained. But this book is meant only to excite your interest, not to satisfy it. It is essential that the list of recommended books you will find at the end of this Preface should be ordered for your class library before you begin the year, so that right from the start you may learn how and where to look for fuller information on any subject. Then once a week, perhaps, the Teacher can use one of the suggested questions at the back of the book to test how well you have in fact covered the ground.

A word of warning about dates. For reasons to which I refer in the early chapters, many of the dates given in this book are approximate, not exact. Every month fresh facts about our history are unearthed; and one of the Teacher's vital tasks as he uses this book is to read periodicals such as *The Journal of African History* and *Notes Africaines*, so as to keep his teaching material up to date, checked constantly against the findings of recent research. He will also find the periodicals published by the University Colleges and Universities in West Africa of increasing interest in this respect.

I acknowledge gratefully the kindness of Professor William Leo Hansberry, Professor of African History at Howard University, in showing me chronological lists of rulers, compiled during a lifetime of painstaking research; and in being so patient with me.

Pupils and teachers are asked to regard the time charts as a supplement to the text, not as a substitute for it; for otherwise false conclusions are certain to be drawn. And the addition of other related events has deliberately been left as a project for each class.

I have used the word 'civilized' in the text. To me it simply means 'having achieved mastery over the forces of nature and the instincts of man'. It does *not* necessarily mean '*Western* civilization'. Its opposite is 'primitive'.

Volumes 1 and 2 are together intended to cover the new History of West Africa syllabus for the G.C.E. of the West African Examinations Council. This considerably revised edition has been prepared with this in view. Where there are alternative spellings I have endeavoured to follow the form which the pupil will meet in the examination paper, and this applies in particular to *Asante* in place of the usual *Ashanti*.

SUGGESTED LIST FOR CLASS LIBRARY: J. D. Fage, *An Atlas of African History* and *An Introduction to the History of West Africa*; R. J. Wingfield, *The Story of old Ghana, Melli and Songhai*; E. W. Bovill, *The Golden Trade of the Moors*; B. Davidson, *The Lost Cities of Africa*. (Pages 344 to 348 of the latter book contain further suggestions.)

W.C.

CONTENTS

Map 1 Some Land and Sea Routes

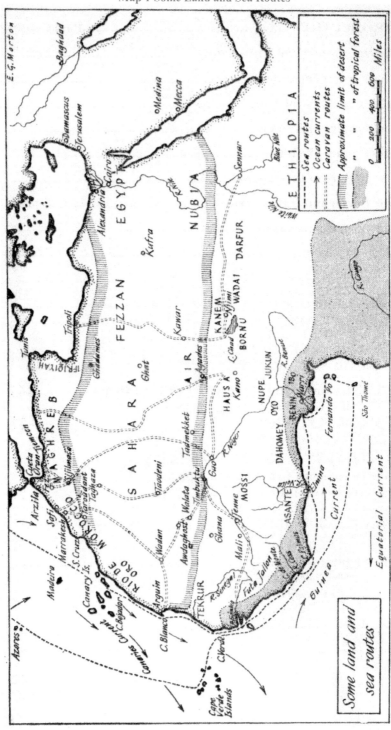

Some land and sea routes

PLATES

MAPS

Part One: Before the Europeans

1

The Earliest Inhabitants

This book tells a story. It is a true story, and I hope that you will also find it an exciting one. It is the story of how the way of life of men and women in West Africa has changed gradually since man first began to live here about 500,000 years ago. As we shall see, these changes were slow at first, and were not even continuous. Today, however, they are both continuous and rapid.

Five hundred thousand years is a very long time, even in the history of a people. So the changes you will read about are very great. At the *beginning* of our story, our people were probably hardly able even to speak. They lived lives very much like those of animals. They did not belong to groups such as tribes and families, or live in communities such as towns and villages. They led solitary lives for most of the time; that was why speech as we know it was unnecessary to them. Food and drink were their main need.

At the *end* of our story, we shall find our people able to talk about and ask for complicated things like self-government — so much more difficult to win than mere food and drink. And we have learned today the greatest lesson of all — the art of living together in tribes and nations. If asked what we are, none of us today would think of replying, 'a human being'. We should answer at once, and with pride, 'I am an Ibo', or, 'I am a Nigerian'; 'I am a Twi', or 'I am a Ghanaian'; 'I am a Mandingo' or 'I am a Sierra Leonean'. Unlike those first men and women of our land, we have learnt how to work with and for each other within our communities. We can claim to have developed our own civilization.

Those distant ancestors of ours did not know it, but they had brothers in other parts of our continent, and indeed of our world, who had lived there even longer than our ancestors had lived here. In South and East Africa, for example, men were making stone tools 750,000 years ago. You will probably be curious about two things by now; firstly, how man first 'came into existence' — where he came from in the first place; and secondly, how historians can possibly have discovered these facts about a people who could hardly even speak, let alone write.

I cannot answer your first question, but can stress that all men are brothers, wherever they may live on this earth, sharing the same earliest ancestors. You and I, as students of history, are concerned only with the story of man *after* his appearance on earth. So I must leave it to those who teach you your religion to answer your first question.

Your second question, however, *is* a true historian's question. To understand the answer to it, stop and think for a minute or two of all the things you lost during last term. People have always dropped things accidentally, or left things lying about carelessly, or hidden things somewhere and then forgotten where. Some of these things, like food and clothing, very soon disappear, because some other creature finds them and eats them. But others, like tools, pottery, and coins, which are made of lasting materials, may lie where they have been lost for many centuries. So it is that whilst the story of modern man, as we shall see, is learnt mainly from words he has written down, the story of early man is learnt mainly from objects he has left about carelessly, or secreted away deliberately, and then forgotten all about.

So we find ourselves in the position of detectives searching for clues. We dig carefully in a site where some of these 'relics', as they are called, have already been found. By making a careful note of everything we find, and of exactly where we find it, we can slowly piece together man's story from the very earliest days. And, as you will perhaps realize by now, this kind of historical research (called 'archaeology') can be intensely fascinating at times. At others, of course, it does require a very great deal of laborious, unexciting work.

But I have still not told you how we come to give approximate dates to events which occurred such a long time ago. One way of working out the date of objects we find when we are 'digging up history' is by noting the depth at which the various objects are found. In a mound of relics, which, like a refuse dump, grows higher all the time, the older objects will be at the bottom. In a valley, on the other hand, which grows deeper as time passes, the older relics will be found on the higher slopes.

The Earliest Inhabitants

Fortunately for us, these relics are not scattered all over the surface of our land. They are concentrated in definite sites. This is partly because, as we have seen, man has learnt over many centuries to live together in communities. But another reason is that a particular site will have been chosen originally as a settlement for a reason which still remains after the settlement itself dies out. For example, a hillock may have been chosen as giving good protection against enemies and floods. If, however, a malaria epidemic wipes out the settlement founded on the hillock, sooner or later another community will realize that it too will be safe from enemies and floods on this particular spot. It will build on the ruins of the first community - and so over the centuries will rise the type of 'historical refuse dump' I have just referred to.

The converse will happen in a valley. A small rivulet running through savannah country will offer fertile soil and good watering. The flow of water will wear ever deeper into the soil, and each successive settlement of people will be made a little lower down the slopes of the valley than the previous one. Even if occupation is continuous, the new houses in the village will usually be built as close to the banks of the river as possible without running the risk of flooding. And so there will gradually be created the type of valley I described a moment ago, whose slopes are full of relics which illustrate their owners' history, and the oldest of which are to be found at the top of the slopes.

Following is a diagram of the type of valley which might exist in some part of West Africa where man has not changed too greatly the face of nature. You will notice at once the reference to various 'wet periods'. Over very long periods in our part of Africa, some centuries have brought us much more rain than others just as each year some months bring us more rain than do others. Now a wet period leaves behind quite a different type of soil from that left by a dry period, and this enables us to reconstruct the early past in the way this diagram does.

On the diagram you will also see names given to the 'culture' (that is simply the way of life) of the various peoples who lived on the slopes of this imaginary valley at various periods. Some of the names are rather long, and all will probably be unfamiliar; but you will have to learn them, as they are very important in the early history of our people. However, there was one important result of this constantly changing climate which a diagram like this cannot show.

During wet periods, the forest became very dense, and spread northwards from the coast towards the desert. During the dry periods, it thinned and shrank away again towards the coast. You will notice that 500,000 years ago, West Africans were living through the end of the first wet period. They were using as tools large pebbles, which they sharpened by breaking flakes off along one edge. These primitive tools were useful only for grubbing up wild roots, and perhaps for self-defence.

One hundred thousand years later, at the beginning of the next wet period, we find a different type of tool in use. These stone 'Chellean' tools, as you see they

13

were called, were rather more carefully shaped than had been the pebble tools. Instead of having only one cutting edge, some now had two, meeting at a sharp

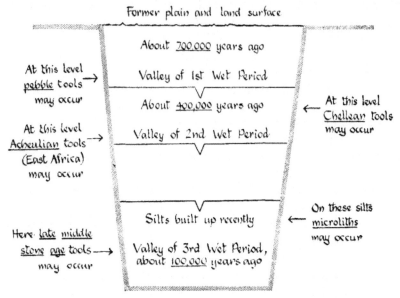

An imaginary valley in Tropical Africa, which has been inhabited for 500,000 years. *With acknowledgments to Dr O. Davies.*

point. Others were ground into sharp blades; yet others were smoothed into balls. The pointed ones could be used for boring holes, the blades perhaps for splitting wood, and the balls for throwing at enemies and prey.

But trouble was on the way for the Chelleans. The continuous heavy rain of the second wet period was making the forest in which they lived ever denser and bigger. Life was becoming more and more difficult as a result. You will realize that the tools I have described left our ancestor of this period very dependent on the weather, on wild plants, and on animals. He could only survive in fairly open country. After all, he hunted, not for fun, but for very life; and even today the hunter, with all his modern weapons, goes to the grasslands and savannah country.

So, as the second wet period dragged on, man was gradually driven northwards from the coast by an advancing green wall of forest. In fact for about 250,000 years he seems to have been forced to leave West Africa altogether, except perhaps near river estuaries and on offshore islands such as the Isles de Los, Plantains, and Sherbro. This period, from about 400,000 to 150,000 years ago, is our 'Dark Ages'. Our culture, built up slowly over a hundred thousand years, was completely destroyed in silent forests dripping under low clouds.

14

The Earliest Inhabitants

This was not so everywhere in Africa. In the East African Lake district, for example, a less unfriendly climate allowed the Chellean culture to develop into the more advanced 'Acheulian' culture, which produced fine axes.

Then, between 150,000 and 100,000 years ago, the sun came out again here in the West. The forest thinned, and human beings came south and west once more.

Amongst the first to return were a people called the 'Sangoans'. Because the objects they left behind are similar to those left behind by the East African Acheulians, we believe that the Sangoan way of life must have spread to West Africa from East Africa. The routes it probably followed are shown on the following pages.

Sangoan man, who lived in West Africa less than 100,000 years ago, was a most interesting person. We know much more about him than we do about those who lived here before him. He used heavy stone tools for digging up roots. He made traps for animals by covering deep pits with foliage. He built rafts and fished from them. And he survived a long time, particularly on the coast. Learning to be more skilful as he went along, he made his tools smaller and smaller.

But unfortunately for him and for us, the rain clouds were gathering again. For the third time, just as West African man was developing his own way of life so successfully, it was almost destroyed by the thickening forests. But this time, not quite. In their last few thousand years here, Sangoan men, like their Chellean predecessors, were forced to move northwards. Some, however, chose to go *south* to the beaches and gravel beds, where they left many tools and weapons which we have found. I do not think their life could have been a very pleasant one, caught between the green devil of the forest to the north and the deep blue sea to the south. But for about 35,000 years (during the last major wet period, lasting from about 50,000 to 15,000 years ago), Sangoan men living, like Man Friday, mainly on the beach, were probably the only human inhabitants of West Africa.

However, it seems that from now on the weather did not swing to quite such extremes again, and so human progress was never again completely reversed. When men *did* eventually return to live all over West Africa once more, they found that quite a broad belt of land, bounded by the Sahara to the north and the Atlantic to the south, was now habitable. A new culture developed now, which we call that of the Late Middle Stone Age. The small knives and scrapers, although still made of stone, were now well enough made to enable their owners to defeat the next wet period without having to move. This period was in any case both a mild and a short one, compared with the previous one. It lasted about 5,000 years, from about 8,000 to 3,000 years ago. Some of these communities had to leave their homes on low ground and take to the hills, it is true. But they were fleeing the floods, not the forest.

15

Map 2 The Spread of Sangoan Culture. *With acknowledgements to Dr. O. Davies.*

Our forefathers had now become so skilful that they no longer needed to work with bulky tools. So we find in this Late Middle Stone Age 'microliths' being used. This word means very small stone tools. They were made of a hard stone called quartz, and could be delicately shaped exactly as required. They could be stuck into arrow heads, or into the ends of sticks used for cutting or scraping.

A still finer way of life developed next, which we call the 'Neolithic' or New Stone Age. The Neolithic West African had become master of the materials he was using to make his tools and weapons. But in addition he was making pottery. This is always a sign that a community is leading a fairly settled life, since pottery is both too fragile and too heavy to carry long distances. It is also a sign that permanent huts were now being built here for the first time, perhaps of clay or mud, perhaps of sticks.

If we stop for a moment to see when our brothers elsewhere reached a similar stage of development, we find that Egyptians were making pottery about 6,000 years ago, the Europeans and Asians about 1,000 years later. Our first pottery in West Africa dates from about 4,000 years ago.

But Neolithic man here, as well as discovering the new 'plastic' art of pottery, did many other things. He made axes from the greenstone which is still so common here, and which takes such a good edge. These axes were probably similar in shape to those still in use today in some parts of New Guinea. He bored holes in round stones, making them look rather like the doughnuts that are sold in our large towns today. Some of these stones may have been used as beads. Others, however, were much too heavy and large for that. These had large centre holes, and so were probably used to slip over the handles of the stone axes I have just mentioned, in order to make their heads heavier. This is still done by Bushmen in South-West Africa today.

If we are right in believing that beads were used as ornaments by Neolithic men — or rather women — here, then they had discovered by now beauty as well as usefulness. This is another important milestone in the development of a people's way of life. Historians used to think that early West Africans did not know how to make beautiful objects. But recently some very old and very beautiful pottery work in the shape of human heads has been discovered in the valleys of the Niger and the Benue just above their confluence, i.e. the point where the rivers meet. The first of these was found near Nok, a village in the Zaria province of Northern Nigeria; so they are called the Nok figurines. The people who made them we now believe to have lived in that region between 900 B.C. and A.D. 200. It is also almost certain that the people living in Central Nigeria today are the direct descendants of those distant artists.

The people who made the figurines found at Nok were not only artists who loved beauty. They were also craftsmen who knew how to mine and work iron. At the height of their civilization, probably just before the birth of Christ, they thus led West Africans out of the Stone Age and into the Metal Age — a vital passage. For useful as other metals were, it was the knowledge of ironwork that was to give to all primitive people the key to progress.

Yet you must never forget the terrible handicaps which the first West Africans had to overcome to progress even so far. The climatic changes in Europe, alternately warm and cold, had merely made life there difficult, and so had acted as a spur to the inventiveness of the inhabitants. The climatic changes here, alternately wet and dry, had from time to time made human life quite impossible. The hands of our clock had not merely been stopped by unkind nature; but again and again they had been turned right back.

It is hardly surprising, then, that we entered our Neolithic Age, as we have seen, about 2,000 years after the Egyptians; nor is it surprising that whilst our European cousins were emerging from their Neolithic Age and entering their Bronze Age about 3,000 years ago, we in West Africa had then only just entered our Neolithic Age. You will have noticed, however, how small the gap between us and the Egyptians and Europeans was when seen against the whole length of human history - 700,000 years or more.

I have had to use words like 'probably', 'about', and 'we believe' rather often in this first chapter, because when we are talking about the very distant past we can never be absolutely certain of our facts and dates. But if you possibly can, do visit a museum and see for yourself actual examples of the tools, pottery, weapons and ornaments of which I have been writing.

2

Africa in Classical Times[1]

You will remember how I mentioned in the last chapter[2] that we are all brothers in one vast family, the family of man. Now it may seem to you that, as time goes on, this family is breaking up into ever smaller parts. This is quite true *politically*, that is in the way we are governed. There are more self-governing nations in the world today (over 100) than there have ever been, and their number is likely to continue to increase. The Roman Empire and the British Empire are only two of the many large groups out of which dozens of separate states have been created.

But *culturally*, that is in the way we live, the human family has drawn closer together throughout its history, slowly at first, and now with increasing speed. Two thousand years ago, the way of life of a citizen of Rome was completely different from that of a citizen of, say, Zaria. Today, in both Rome and Zaria you will find people who dance to jazz music, profess Christianity, study in a university, and find that life is very difficult when their telephone is out of order. The rhythms of jazz originated amongst Africans; Christianity, like so many other great religions, sprang up amongst Asians; the idea of a university was conceived by Europeans; and the telephone was developed by an American. Yet all four now belong to the world, and to the common cultural heritage of the family of man. The rest of this book is really an account of the way in which our people here in West Africa have gradually contributed more and more to, and benefited more and more from, that common heritage.

---

[1] In the days of the Greek and Roman Empires, about 400 B.C. to AD. 400.
[2] p. 12

West Africa in History

Fifty centuries ago, when the scattered tribes of Europe were still illiterate and barbarous, there lived in a fertile river valley in the north-east corner of our continent a people who had a very advanced civilization. That river was the Nile, and the people were the Egyptians. Very few of them were negroes; and, fascinating as it is, we cannot stop to study that civilization here. It has, however, one lesson to teach which I must refer to at this stage of our study.

It is that the finest civilizations have usually sprung from the most fertile soils, almost literally. Men's culture is rooted in their land. Each summer the Nile valley becomes a shallow lake, whose receding waters leave behind a layer of extremely fertile silt. It is not surprising, therefore, that many adventurous people from both Asia and Africa (including, quite possibly, some negroes) converged on this valley, which was conveniently placed near the land bridge linking the two continents. Intermingling, they formed a new race with relatively few material worries, and so plenty of leisure to give to other things. They painted the walls of their caves, some of them with negro subjects. They built the Sphinx and the Pyramids. And they produced a supreme achievement when they taught themselves to write in a kind of picture language called hieroglyphics.

Not far away from Egypt, in Mesopotamia, was to be found another great home of early civilization. Here too we find that the roots sank into fertile riverain soil, which had attracted energetic people. Mesopotamia, 'the country between the rivers', lies, green and rich, between the Euphrates and the Tigris. In about the twentieth century before Christ, it was occupied by a people called the Sumerians. They developed an early form of writing too, using wedge-shaped letters called 'cuneiform' letters, after the Latin word 'cuneus' - a wedge.

Neither of these two highly civilized peoples was negro. The people of West Africa, on the other hand, nearly all belong to the negro race. Negroes are the original natives of the African continent. Today they share it with many non-negro people. Some, like the Jews of North Africa and the Berbers of North-West Africa, have lived on the continent for at least 5,000 years. Others, like the Arabs who are now to be found all along the north coast, did not cross the land bridge from Asia to Africa until the seventh century A.D. and later. Yet others, like the Europeans of Algeria, South Africa, and East and Central Africa, have entered our continent only during the past few hundred years. The negroes alone, who are today found in large numbers between latitudes 18° and 4° N, and particularly in the western end of that strip, cannot be proved ever to have entered Africa as a race, either by sea or land. They have apparently always been here. And it is that western end of that strip, in which our race is massed, that we call today West Africa.

However, the West African negro has had his history and way of life very greatly changed by the non-negro people with whom he has come into contact. Some of these have reached our country overland, others have come from overseas. All have left their mark on us. Unfortunately, a heavy curtain hangs over much of our history before these contacts with foreign peoples began. In spite of the difficult climate to which I have referred, and the absence of river valleys as fertile as those which supported the civilizations of Egypt and Mesopotamia, our ancestors were able to produce the Nok figurines 2,000 years ago. But the art of writing, which is the supreme achievement of any civilization, negroes, like Europeans, had to be taught by others. With the exception of the Hausas[1] and the Kotoko tribe from the Lake Chad area, both of whose languages were written with Arabic characters, and the Vai of Liberia, other West African tribes had to wait for the arrival of Europeans before learning to record their words on paper.

Travel is easy in Europe, and difficult in Africa. So even this new literacy, once taught, spread quickly in the former continent, but slowly in the latter, before modern times brought the defeat of the tropical forest and desert by the train, the car, and the aeroplane. Thus it happens that we must look to the writings of others to lift the curtain for us, as we enter modern times.

This method of discovering the early history of our people is not of course as satisfactory as using the written records of a people themselves. Provided however that we constantly check and cross-check what we read against what archaeology has to tell us, we can learn a great deal from the accounts of foreign travellers to our lands. We must also of course compare what these accounts contain with what we know of West African life today, and try to trace lines of development.

The Greeks and Romans of classical times were amongst the first of these travellers. They were very careful to distinguish between the negro and the non-negro inhabitants of Africa. Herodotus, for example, uses the term 'Ethiopians' for all the inhabitants of Africa outside Egypt. But he makes a further division. 'The Ethiopians,' he writes, 'from the direction of the sunrising (for the Ethiopians were in two bodies) were in no way different in appearance from the other Ethiopians, but in their language and in the nature of their hair only: for the Ethiopians from the East are straight-haired, but those of Libya have hair more thick and woolly than that of any other men.' By 'Libya' here we know Herodotus meant Africa south and west of Egypt.

He then describes the voyage of certain Phoenician sailors round 'Libya'. 'They set forth from the Erythraian Sea[2] and sailed through the Southern Sea; and when autumn came, they would put to shore and sow the land, wherever in Libya they might happen to be as they sailed, and then they waited for the harvest: and having reaped the corn they would sail on, so that after two years had elapsed, in the third year they turned through the Pillars of Hercules and arrived again in

---

[1] p. 56
[2] i.e. the Red Sea and Indian Ocean round the East African coasts.

Egypt. And they reported a thing which I cannot believe, but another man may, namely that in sailing round Libya they had the sun on their right hand.'

You will see at once that this early (perhaps first) circumnavigation of Africa must have been done in a clock-wise direction. And the fact that the historian who recorded it for us notes that the sun was on the ship's starboard side for much of the time, even though he finds it incredible, encourages us to go on and read further.

A certain Sataspes, he tells us, was sentenced by his king, Xerxes of Persia, to circumnavigate Africa as a penance for a sin he had committed. He did not complete the journey; but he did report seeing 'at the furthest point which he reached . . . a dwarfish people, who used clothing made from the palm tree, and who, whenever they' (Sataspes' crew) 'came to land with their ship, left their town and fled to the mountains'.

Herodotus' longest and most interesting account of Africa, however, is contained in his description of an overland expedition, not a sea voyage. This expedition was the third sent out by King Cambyses of Persia, in about 520 B.C. Its members were trying to reach the land of 'the long-lived Ethiopians by the Southern Sea'. Cambyses decided first to send spies to this unknown land, 'both to see whether the table of the Sun existed really, which is said to exist among the Ethiopians, and in addition to spy out all else, but pretending to be bearers of gifts for their king. . . . So when Cambyses had resolved to send the spies, forthwith he sent for . . . men . . . who understood the Ethiopian tongue. . . . He sent them to the Ethiopians, enjoining them what they should say and giving them gifts to bear with them, that is to say a purple garment, and a collar of twisted gold with bracelets, and an alabaster box of perfumed ointment, and a jar of palm-wine. Now these Ethiopians to whom Cambyses was sending are said to be the tallest and most beautiful of all men; and besides other customs which they are reported to have different from other men, there is especially this, it is said, with regard to the royal power - whomsoever of the men of their nation they judge to be the tallest and to have strength in proportion to his stature, this man they appoint to reign over them. So when they had come to this people, they presented their gifts to the king who ruled over them, and at the same time they said as follows: "The king of the Persians, Cambyses, desiring to become a friend and guest to thee, sent us with a command to come to speech with thee, and he gives thee for gifts these things which he himself most delights to use." The Ethiopian, however, perceiving that they had come as spies, spoke to them as follows: "Neither did the King of the Persians send you bearing gifts because he thought it a matter of great moment to become my guest-friend, nor do ye speak true things (for ye come as spies of my kingdom), nor again is he a righteous man; for if he had been righteous he would not have coveted a land other than his own, nor would he be leading away into slavery men at whose hands he has received no wrong. Now however give him this bow and speak to him these words: The King of the Ethiopians gives this counsel to the King of the Persians, that when the Persians draw their bows (of equal size to mine) as easily as I do this, then he should march against the long-lived Ethiopians, provided he be superior to them in numbers; but until that time he should feel gratitude to the gods that they do not put it into the mind of the sons of the Ethiopians to acquire another land in addition to their own."'

Even through this old translation you will gain a vivid impression of the respect in which the 'Ethiopians' were held not only by the Persians, but by the writer. There is certainly no suggestion here that Cambyses had sent his envoys to 'civilize' an inferior people. We do not know just how far into Africa these travellers in fact went. It is most unlikely that they reached what today we call West Africa. But we can see at once that it was a negro kingdom they were describing, and that it was well to the west of the then known lands of Africa. 'As one passes beyond the place of the midday,' Herodotus writes elsewhere, 'the Ethiopian land is that which extends furthest of all inhabited land towards the sunset. This produces both gold in abundance and huge elephants and trees of all kinds growing wild, and ebony, and men who are of all men the tallest, the most beautiful, and the most long-lived.' He goes on to claim that eighteen of the 330 Egyptian kings were of 'Ethiopian' race.

There were later classical writers about negro kingdoms, however, who had a less flattering tale to tell. Strabo, who lived in Italy at the time of Christ, and 400 years after Herodotus the Greek, states that 'above Mauretania, on the exterior sea, is the country of the western Ethiopians, as they are called, which for the most part is badly inhabited'. He goes on to mention camels, leopards, rhinoceroses, elephants, and an abundance of huge bamboos in this distant land. Although the people's hair is curly, Strabo thinks that in other respects they resemble the people of the south of India. He adds: 'They at present lead for the most part a wandering life, and are destitute of the means of subsistence, on account of the barrenness of the soil, the disadvantage of the climate, and their great distance from us. Now the contrary is the case with the Egyptians in all these respects. . . . The Ethiopians are wretched, mostly naked, wandering with small flocks of sheep, goats and oxen; they have dogs that are fierce but small, and it is rumoured that some amongst the people are pygmies. They live on millet and barley, from which a drink is prepared, but they have no oil, and use butter and fat. There are no fruits except in royal gardens; some of the people eat grass, twigs, lotus, roots of reeds, flesh and blood of animals, milk and cheese. They defy their kings, who are kept shut up in palaces. Their capital is called Meroe.'

We know that the ruins of Meroe are on the Nile, a hundred miles below Khartoum. So clearly Strabo is describing the *East* African negro, whereas Herodotus' reference to the sun set may mean that his travellers had explored much further west than Strabo's. We do not know for sure. But let us glance, finally, at the writings of a still later historian of classical times. Caius Plinius Secundus lived from A.D. 23 to A.D. 79, and visited Africa himself in A.D. 44. Pliny, as he is usually called, calls his encyclopaedia boldly *Historia Naturalis* - 'an Account of countries, nations, seas, towns, havens, mountains, rivers, distances, and people who now exist or formerly existed'. 'If we pass through the interior of Africa in a southerly direction,' he tells us, 'we shall find, first of all, the Liby-Egyptians. . . . Beyond these are the Nigritae, nations of Ethiopia, so-called from the River Nigris. . . . The opinion of those is exceedingly well founded who place two Aethiopias beyond the deserts of Africa, and more particularly that expressed by Homer, who tells us that the Aethiopians are divided into two nations, those of the east and those of the west. The River Nigris has the same characteristics as the Nile; it produces papyrus and just the same animals, and it rises at the same seasons of the year.'

It may have been this particular passage that misled the European explorers of the nineteenth century into believing that the Niger might be a tributary of the Nile. In fact Pliny may not have been referring to the West African river we know at all. He goes on to mention the existence of pygmies amongst the 'Aethiopians', saying that 'they dwell amongst the marshes, in which the River Nile takes its rise'. Amongst the other tribes he describes are a people who are of a black tint, but stain the body all over with a kind of red earth. . . .' Their land 'is situate in a southern hemisphere, forests of ebony are to be seen of the brightest verdure; and in the midst of these regions there is a mountain of immense height, which overhangs the sea and emits a perpetual flame, and at a distance of four days' sail from it is a promontory, known as Hesperu Ceras'.

'Hesperu Ceras' is almost certainly Cape Verde, modern historians believe. There is also a river called the 'Bambotus', which Pliny places in the west of the land of the Ethiopians, and which he states is full of crocodiles and hippopotami.

These glimpses of Africa in classical times are very tantalizing, partly because they are so fleeting, partly because we do not know exactly what parts of the continent they are unveiling to us, and partly because, mixed in with what we know from modern West African life are accurate descriptions, we find some fantastic untruths - accounts in Pliny of 'men who do not live beyond their fortieth year', for example. If we bear in mind who wrote them and when they were written, however, these travellers' tales of classical times can provide us with a useful background against which to study in more detail the West Africa of more recent times.

3

The Empire of Ghana

The Empire of Ghana came into existence in about A.D. 300. The first reference to it we have been able to find was made by an Arab astronomer called Al-Fazari in the eighth century, and it was first marked on a map in 830. It was finally destroyed in A.D. 1240.

Ghana was a negro empire. Some history books may give you the impression that, because for brief periods of its history it fell under the rule of non-negro people, it was therefore not a true negro state. Such an impression would be false. Most of the people of the Empire were Soninkes, members of the very large Mande-speaking group of negro tribes. Moreover the Empire was self-governing during nearly the whole of its existence. The fact that between 1076 and 1088 it was ruled by Berbers does not make it a Berber state, any more than the fact that the Gold Coast was ruled by Britain from 1821 to 1957 makes modern Ghana a British state.

The name 'Ghana' was originally the title of an Emperor, like 'Alafe' or 'Alafin'. It was later also used as the name of his court, the place from which he ruled. This court was not necessarily always in the same town. For much of the period of the Empire's existence the court was in a town called Koumbi. But it is important to remember that the boundaries of neither capital nor Empire were as firmly fixed as are those of modern cities and states.

From the fourth century onwards the camel was increasingly used by the Berbers of North Africa as a means of transport in the trade across the Sahara. As an indirect result of this use of the camel, the Muslims spread in increasing numbers in the late seventh century, and many of the pagans in the Empire were converted to Islam.

The Empire was very rich in gold, which was the main commodity of that trade. Many Arab writers bear witness to this wealth. Al-Fazari, whom I have already mentioned, called Ghana simply 'the land of gold'. Al-Masudi, writing in Baghdad in the tenth century, says that Ghana's gold was actually 'visible on the

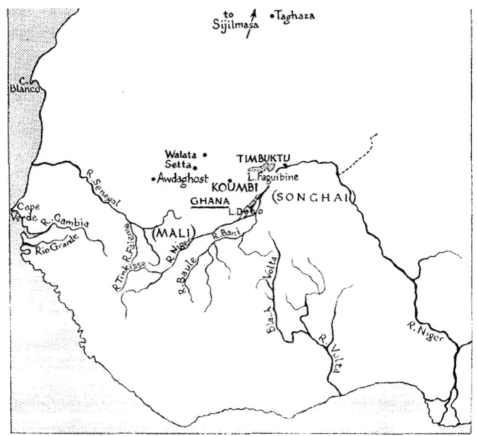

Map 3 The Empire of Ghana (about A.D. 300-1240)

ground'. Ibn Hawqal, a traveller from Baghdad to Ghana in the early 970s, called the Emperor of Ghana 'the richest in the world because of his gold'; and in those days Baghdad was a city whose people were in touch with many parts of Europe, Asia, and North Africa. About 100 years after lbn Hawqal's time Al-Bakri confirms eloquently that Ghana was extremely rich. He had never visited Africa - his home was in Cordoba in Spain - but he was obviously a man who had read widely. He tells us how gold was to be found everywhere in the Ghana court - in the Emperor's cap (how this reminds us of the modern Ghanaian chief!), the horses' trappings, the pages' swords and shields. Yet another hundred

26

years and Al-Gharnati, another Arab author, tells us (in about 1162) that salt in Ghana was sometimes worth more than its weight in gold, for the latter was as plentiful as the former was scarce. The most striking reference to the wealth of Ghana, however, had been made just eight years before this, in a geography written by Idrisi in 1154. Idrisi tells us that the Emperor of Ghana tethered his horse to a nugget of pure gold weighing thirty pounds. Even if, as Al-Bakri had told us earlier, the horses of Ghana were small, and the Emperor had a monopoly of all nuggets (the people having to be content with gold dust), we cannot fail to be impressed that so much gold could be spared for so lowly a purpose. We shall come across other references to this particular nugget later, so there seems little doubt that Idrisi was writing the truth. Besides gold, there was silk in Ghana, the Emperor wearing a mantle of this expensive Oriental material.

But iron was in some ways an even more important mineral to the people of Ghana than gold. We do not know whether they learnt the craft of ironwork from the people who made the Nok figurines, and who seem to have been scattered at one time in many different parts of West Africa. But certainly El Zhouri, another Arab writer, notes that before 1150 the people of the Empire of Ghana were successfully attacking with swords and lances other peoples 'who know not iron and fight with bars of ebony'. I have already referred[1] to the great advantages which a people who have both the ore and the skill for making iron weapons and implements possesses over others.

Where then was this fabulous negro state? We do not know for certain, except that it lay to the west of the great northern most bend of the Niger. However, an archaeologist has discovered, 205 miles north of Bamako, the ruins of a large town. There are several reasons why we believe this to have been the capital of the Empire, at least during part of its existence. First of all, the name of the area today is 'Koumbi Saleh', and we know that the Empire's capital was for a time a city called Koumbi. Secondly, the local sheiks at once took the archaeologist to this spot in 1913 when he asked them to show him the site of ancient Ghana. You will know from your own experience how often correct historical information is preserved in West Africa in local unwritten form. Thirdly, ten miles away from Koumbi Saleh were found ruins of another town known locally as 'Ghanata' and which, unlike those of Koumbi itself, contain no stone. And all around Koumbi are ancient graves.

Now 900 years ago Al-Bakri had written of just two such towns as comprising together Ghana's capital. One, he wrote, was a Muslim town with twelve mosques and a good supply of fresh water and vegetables. The other was the royal town, called Al-Ghaba by the Muslims, with stone and wooden houses protected by a town wall, and a single mosque for visiting Muslim diplomats. Al-Bakri even mentions that the land between the two towns was covered with

---

[1]P. 17

houses - a kind of 'ribbon development', perhaps, such as we have along the main roads on the outskirts of some of our towns today. Indeed, the only puzzling fact is that Al-Bakri's account speaks of six miles instead of ten between the twin towns. But then even this depends on what he regarded as the centres of the towns.

It is, however, almost certain that the Emperor's capital was in different places at different times. Another probable site was Setta, eighty miles south-west of Walata. Yet another, this time suggested by the geographer Idrisi, was on a large river (he calls it the Nile, but almost certainly means either the Niger or the Senegal). This river-side site was probably one of the last sites occupied by the capital.

As to the form of government in the Empire, this also probably varied from time to time. But when the Empire was at the height of its power, in the tenth and eleventh centuries, this government was extremely efficiently administered. There were both a court of appeal and a court of justice, the latter sitting in a chamber not far from the mosque we have noticed in the royal town. There was a Cabinet of imperial ministers, the majority of whom at the time Al-Bakri was writing were Muslims (though this does not necessarily mean that they were not negroes). There was an official to manage the imperial 'territory' or land. There was a Governor set over the whole capital, whilst the Muslim section had its own imams and muazzins, and its full-time Koran readers. The Emperor had flags and a personal standard which was carried before him as he rode round his capital to receive petitions. Various wild animals were driven ahead of the imperial procession, no doubt to impress on everyone the Emperor's might. What really kept his subjects (who included, says Al-Masudi, some petty kings) in obedience was the fact, recorded by Al-Bakri, that the Emperor could at one time put 200,000 men in the field of battle, of whom 40,000 were bowmen.

All of this elaborate machinery of government was paid for out of the Empire's very prosperous trade. In the tenth century a donkey load of salt entering Ghana was worth £100 to £150 in gold. The Emperor contented himself with taking 10s worth of gold from every merchant leading a donkey loaded with salt into the capital, and £1 worth of gold from every merchant leading a donkey out of it loaded with gold. The duty on copper was 5/8 oz. per load, and on general merchandise 1 1/4oz. of gold per load. The northern terminus for this trade was Sijilmasa in Morocco.

The social customs of the people of the Empire are full of interest to us in West Africa today, as they bear so much resemblance to our own. Since most of those people were pagans, they worshipped idols in sacred groves, under the direction of priests. The royal tombs were also in these groves; and buried with each king were his ornaments, weapons, vessels, carpets, cushions, mats, and even the servants who had served his meals. Victims were sacrificed to the dead, and libations containing alcohol were poured to appease or enlist the support of the spirits of the ancestors, just as is done today.

Al-Bakri tells us that of the non-Muslims in the Empire in the eleventh century only the Emperor and his heir (usually his sister's son) were allowed to wear sewn clothes. Other non- Muslims wore lengths of cotton, silk or brocade cloth. But 100 years later, according to Idrisi, their clothing consisted of robes, loin-cloths, and mantles, each citizen dressing according to his means. The same writer tells us that, at the time when their capital was astride a great river, the citizens used strongly made boats both for fishing and as ferries. Their houses, at least the more wealthy, were not only well built of stone and wood, but also well decorated. Idrisi mentions that the Emperor had sculptures and paintings in his castle; and since these works of art were well lit the castle also had glass windows - no doubt the members of the Emperor's court were able both to enjoy looking at and to seek to match their monarch's taste in art. We must not forget, however, that this particular castle was not built until 1116, towards the end of the Empire's long existence. Former Emperors may not all have lived in such luxury.

What we are reminded of throughout the Empire's existence is the determination of its people to defend their land from attack, at all costs. In the tenth century Al-Masudi, like other Arab historians, describes a most interesting method they used of peaceful self-defence:

'The kingdom of Ghana is one of great importance, and it adjoins the land of the gold mines. Great peoples of the land of the negroes live there. They have traced a boundary which no one who sets out to them ever crosses. When the merchants reach this boundary, they place their wares and cloth on it and then depart. The owners of the merchandise then return, and if they are satisfied with what they have found, they take it. If not, they go away again, and the negroes return and add to the price until the bargain is struck.'

You will remember, too, Al-Bakri's reference to a defensive town wall,[1] and Idrisi calls the Emperor's palace a castle. Clearly these are people who know they have something worth taking a lot of trouble to protect. They kept tame animals, including dogs 'of excellent pedigree', the small horses already mentioned, and the elephants and giraffes we found at the head of the imperial procession. The reference to the Emperor being succeeded by his sister's son will remind many of us of our own customary inheritance laws. Then we read that the Emperor's subjects greeted him by clapping their hands. School-children in some parts of West Africa are still taught to use this method of announcing their arrival to their elders - outside a staff-room door, for example. These similarities are evidence that some modern West Africans are the direct descendants of the people of the Empire of Ghana.

---

[1] p. 27

We cannot say definitely either where these people came from originally, nor exactly where they all went. Mande-speaking people are found today in many parts of West Africa; but they are concentrated in and around the borders of Guinea in the greatest numbers. The Mende people, Sierra Leone's largest tribe, also have Mande-speaking ancestors, and many Mende chiefs even today are Mandingos. Moreover, there are many Mende customs which remind us strongly of the customs of the people of the Empire of Ghana. The Mendes have a secret society called the Porro, which has its own secret groves. The Empire of Ghana, Al-Bakri tells us, had its 'woods and copses where live the . . . men in charge of the religious cult', guarded so that no unauthorized person could enter. On the other hand there are important differences. A Mende chief is usually succeeded by his own eldest son, not by his sister's Thus the most we can say confidently at present is that the citizens of ancient Ghana were pure negroes who must have come originally from a part of West Africa where the Mande group of languages was spoken, and that they probably dispersed to various parts of West Africa on the collapse of the Empire, taking their customs with them. This collapse came as a result of repeated attacks by the many enemies on the Empire's borders. These attacks must have started very soon after Ghana reached the height of its fame, and its great wealth was the attraction. A historian called Abderrahman as-Sadi, writing in Timbuktu in 1652, says that there were twenty-two kings of Ghana before 622, and twenty-two after, and that they were all 'white men'. He may be right in his figures; he is certainly mistaken in saying that all Ghana's kings were non-negro. But the fact that such a mistake could have been made by someone living not far from the probable boundaries of the Empire only 400 years after its collapse shows how well known was the foreign interest Ghana attracted throughout its existence. As early as the ninth century Berber tribesmen's attacks were being fought off by the warriors of the young Empire. In the following century Awdaghost, the chief trading centre of one of these Berber tribes, was actually paying tribute to Ghana. But by the middle of the eleventh century the strength of the Berbers had greatly increased. The Emperor of Ghana was still a powerful ruler, loyally served. Basi, the Emperor at this time, inspired so much loyalty that, according to Al-Bakri, though he was blind his ministers pretended that he could see, prompting him secretly what to say. Taking no chances, however, he wisely said only, 'This is good', or, 'This is bad', when shown objects! Basi was friendly towards the Muslims in his capital. Were his successors less wise in this respect? We do not know. Anyhow in 1072 Basi was succeeded by Tankamanin; and four years later the Almoravid Berbers, who had recaptured Awdaghost in 1055, at last captured Koumbi — just ten years, incidentally, after the Normans invaded Britain.

Whilst the Norman conquest of Britain was to prove permanent, however, the Almoravid conquest of Ghana was on this occasion to prove only temporary. The conquerors were looking, not for new homes, but for fresh spoils. They were not a single tribe, but a group of fierce North African nomads who kept together only as long as it suited them for purposes of defence or attack. Abu Bekr, the leader who captured Koumbi in 1076, seems to have been a gifted soldier. But even he had had great difficulty in keeping his spirited followers together. In 1062 he

P. 2 A house which has been excavated on the probable site of the last capital of the ancient empire of Ghana

had had to watch the northern wing of the Almoravid army break away from his command, under the leadership of his own cousin, Yusuf. The southern wing was the one that captured Koumbi, whose citizens were now forced to pay tribute to their new rulers until 1088.

So rich a city attracted fresh enemies as soon as the wandering Almoravids moved on, however; even though it was probably rebuilt now on another site. In 1203 it was defeated again, this time by a Susu ruler, Sumanguru. As usual, the conqueror levied heavy taxes from the conquered; but by now the traders of Koumbi had had enough. Many of them moved north to Walata in 1224 to avoid paying these taxes. They moved just in time, for fresh trouble was ahead. In 1240 Sumanguru was himself defeated and killed, as we shall learn, by Sundiata, ruler of one of his own vassal states, Mali. Koumbi was now in no condition to resist anyone. Some of the remaining inhabitants, tradition relates, had fled before a drought, yet others on the death of a snake which was regarded as housing the city's guardian spirit. Now its military guardian and conqueror, Sumanguru, was also dead; and it lay defenceless and exposed. Who delivered its death blow we are not sure - it may have been Sundiata himself, or one of his generals, or just a band of roving soldiers looking for spoils. In any case in 1240 the once rich and powerful capital of the Empire of Ghana was completely destroyed.

4

The Empire of Mali

Istory has twice linked the names 'Ghana' and 'Mali'. We saw at the end of the last chapter how Sumanguru, the Susu conqueror of Ghana, was himself defeated and killed by Sundiata, Emperor of Mali, in A.D. 1240. Today, more than 700 years later, we have watched the two names being revived in two adjacent and newly independent states.

The Empire of Mali has been described by a modern historian, writing in 1959, as 'one of the greatest states in the world of its time'. It did not reach this position until after it had conquered Ghana and the Susu, and Sundiata was only one of the many builders of the Empire's strength. His great achievement was to unite the many tribes within the Empire's borders under one centralized rule. He thus laid the foundations of Mali's greatness. Sundiata is remembered amongst the descendants of his people as a sickly child, lame as a result of some form of paralysis. This sickness was to be a blessing in disguise to the child, however. For the all-conquering Susu king Sumanguru, whom we met at the end of the last chapter, spared his life out of pity for his condition, although he killed some of his brothers and sisters. We are told how the handicapped child used to crawl on all fours to steal food, but when caught, would fight like a lion.

Fortune tellers had predicted a great future for this child, and we can imagine his parents' disappointment when he did not even walk until he was seven years old. It was at this age that he lost his father, Maghan Kon Fatta, King of Mali. Sundiata's eldest brother, Dankaran Touman, succeeded to the throne. Lovingly cared for by the royal staff, Sundiata gradually recovered the use of his legs, and grew stronger daily. Soon he was famous at court as a warrior and hunter, and, like all successful athletes, he became very popular. This popularity aroused the envy of the King (his brother); and Sundiata in the end had to flee from the Mali capital, Niani, with his mother, a sister, and a brother. The King's hatred pursued them so far that no Mandingo village would shelter them.

Emperor Sumanguru also seems to have sensed somehow that the young Sundiata was someone to be feared. When the fleeing prince sought refuge in Tabo, the capital of the ruling family of Futa, Sumanguru ordered this family, who were also his vassals, to expel him. The same thing happened at another capital, Djeliba, south-west of Niani, and at the court of the ruler of the now very much weakened kingdom of Ghana. It was Tounkara, king of the Meama near Lake Faguibine, who finally gave the exiles asylum. Sumanguru must have been a formidable ruler!

But this great Emperor's rule was now drawing near its end. A revolt of all Mandingos suddenly exploded, set off by the Emperor's pitiless 'taxation' which consisted of depriving the Mandingos of their most beautiful women, as well as their food and gold. When Sumanguru gathered his army to suppress the revolt, the Mali Emperor took fright and fled, having heard that Sumanguru had powers of witchcraft. Thus it was left to Sundiata, the formerly crippled child, and now a prince in exile, to fight the tyrant. A delegation from the Mandingo rebels persuaded the King of the Meama to give Sundiata (whose military skill and courage were now well known in the area) an army.

One sad blow befell the brave young man on the eve of his departure to face his frightening foe. His mother died. Although stricken with grief, Sundiata only stayed long enough to bury her, and the very next day he marched with the brother who had shared his exile, against Sumanguru. They re-entered Mandingo country among much excitement and rejoicing, and their army grew stronger daily. These two brothers had become fast friends during their exile, and we may be sure that their initial affection and trust in each other was an important factor in their success. King Sesay of Ghana added to the men and arms the Meama king had given them; Kamara Labe, King of Tabo, overcame his fear of Sumanguru sufficiently to place himself under Sundiata's orders. Most important of all, practically all the Mandingo leaders had now rallied to his banner. Finally, the King of Bobo in modern Upper Volta added his contribution of 1,500 archers.

The decisive battle was joined near the village of Krina, which still exists today. As a Mandingo poem says, 'The battle of Krina was terrible'. Sumanguru's defeat was complete, although the Emperor himself was not captured. With his reputation as a sorcerer, of course, he was soon said to have 'disappeared', having been shot with the one weapon which could harm him - an arrow tipped with the spur of a white cock. Legend added that a baobab tree grew on the spot from which he vanished.

The triumphant Sundiata now attacked his defeated enemy's capital, the city of the Susu, which was famed for its 188 strongpoints. After a siege of several months he stormed it. We believe that it was he who then went on to destroy the subject capital of Ghana (Koumbi) also; but he may have sent one of his generals on this comparatively easy mission. In any case, he was now undisputed Emperor of Mali. He did not, in his hour of triumph, forget those who had helped him reach it. All his generals were given military commands within the Empire.

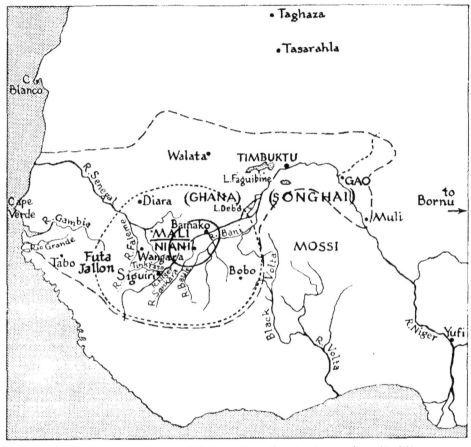

Inner Boundaries: Mali at Sundiata's Accession (1230).
Middle Boundaries: Mali at Sundiata's Death (1255)
Outer Boundaries: Mali at its greatest extent (1350).

Map 4 The Empire of Mali

Sundiata's picture develops as that of a young man with the grit and pluck to overcome a great handicap; affectionate, generous, athletic and brave. The Empire of Mali had a most attractive founder.

After extending the frontiers of Mali until they enclosed all the states forming Sumanguru's defeated Empire (including Ghana), and reached the Atlantic coast to the west of his capital, Sundiata died. He was either shot by an arrow during a

35

public demonstration, or drowned, others say, in the River Sankara near his capital at a spot where sacrifices to his memory are still offered.

The Empire he founded was Muslim, unlike Ghana which was heathen. It was the mediaeval world's chief producer of gold. Its finances were very healthy, and it had a prosperous Berber and Arab merchant class dealing in gold and slaves. Historians of the period contrast the peace of Sundiata's Mali with the warfare which cost Europe and North Africa so much of their wealth at that time. But the peak of Mali's power and fame was probably reached long after his death in 1255, in which year its king first took the proud title of Emperor (Mansa).

The most renowned of the Emperors of Mali was Mansa Kankan Musa, grandson of Sundiata's sister. His fame rests largely on a hadj (pilgrimage) he made to Mecca in 1324, in the course of which he passed through Cairo. Cairo in the fourteenth century was quite as much a cross-roads of the world as Baghdad had been in the tenth century. And yet such was Kankan Musa's display of wealth that the citizens of Cairo were still talking about it a hundred years later. So were the Italians even though he did not visit their country. From 1339 to 1433 a series of their maps marked the position of Mali and depicted its Emperor's wealth.

Musa's successor, Mansa Maghan, allowed the power of the Mali Empire to be reduced greatly. Musa's brother Sulayman, whom we shall be hearing about later in this chapter, was able to restore much of that power before his death in 1359. After this, however, the Empire, torn by internal wars, steadily lost strength and importance; it still remained nevertheless the most important state in West Africa until the rise of the Empire of the Songhai in 1470, and did not entirely disappear until about 1670.

The people of Mali, like those of ancient Ghana, were negroes. Their rulers were of the Mandingo tribe, and many of them had become Mohammedans. As you can tell from the fact that the Emperor himself took the trouble to go on a hadj, Islam was a religion that was very highly valued in Mali. When Kankan Musa met a man whose grandfather had converted Musa's own grandfather to Islam, the Emperor was so pleased that he gave the man a gift of 3,000 mithqals (a mithqal was about 1/8 oz. of gold). All the same, Musa was a very tolerant Muslim, and encouraged the pagan gold-diggers of Wangara to continue to worship their own pagan gods. So you will see that Mali, like Ghana, had a mixture of Mohammedanism and paganism.

But you must not think that there was no military strength behind the Mali Emperor's display of religious zeal and wealth. Whilst Kankan Musa was away on his hadj, his army had not been idle at home. In 1325, led by a brilliant general called Sagaman-dir, it captured the Songhai capital of Gao, and all the broad Songhai land to the north remained subject to Mali for the next fifty years.

Much of our knowledge of the Mali Empire comes from an account of a journey made to it in 1352 - 5. The traveller's full name was Muhammed Ibn

'Abd Allah, but he is usually called Ibn Batuta and he was a Moroccan Arab. One of the things that impressed him most was the fervour with which some of the people of Mali practised Islam. He describes how the ordinary people of the Empire observed with great regularity the hours of prayer, and attended mosque services with their children so faithfully that on Fridays you would find no room left if you arrived late! Worshippers had in fact formed the habit of sending their sons along well ahead of time with their prayer mats, on which the lads knelt (prayerfully, we must hope) to keep their masters' places for them. Even the poorest worshipper would wear clean white clothes on Friday. The Koran was learnt by heart by all, young and old. One child was actually chained until he had memorized it. The feast of Ramadan was observed as carefully in Mali 600 years ago as in modern West Africa. On the night of 27th Ramadan the Emperor would distribute Zakeh (gifts) amongst the preachers and doctors in his court. Even Ibn Batuta, stranger though he was, received on that occasion thirty-three and a third mithqals.

We read, also, of the very strong sense of brotherhood which the Muslims of Mali felt with the rest of the Islamic world. Whilst Ibn Batuta was in the capital the Emperor, who had just recovered from a two-month illness, held a banquet in commemoration of the late Sultan of Morocco. During the banquet reading desks were brought in at which the Koran was read, just as Christian monks used to have portions of the Bible read to them from a little pulpit in their refectory. Then prayers were offered for the Sultan and the Emperor.

As well as the pagans of Wangara, there were many other non-Muslims in Mali. We read of cannibals on its borders; but the impression is definitely created that these were a rarity.

To find the capital of old Mali on a map, follow the Niger up from its estuary, round its great northernmost bend, past Timbuktu and Bamako. You will come to a tributary called the Sankara or Sansara. We believe that the capital of this Empire, a city later called Mali-koro or old Mali, lay somewhere near the confluence of the two rivers. There is again a local tradition in this area that this was so. But unfortunately for us, the local inhabitants believe that the day one of them leads a stranger to the actual site, a terrible disaster will befall them; so it is very difficult to get accurate information from them. By tactful inquiries, however, historians have been able to discover a belief amongst the people living in and near Siguiri, the largest town in the area, that Sundiata took shelter in a village on the Sankara river when in flight from his enemies. It is added that he drowned himself in the river. There are still, in fact, Arab settlers, claiming to be descendants of an Arab community in Mali, living in this region today, particularly in Kela.

But like the capital of Ghana[1] the capital of Mali occupied different sites at different times. The village of Niani near Bamako was a later site, chosen by Sundiata himself. Niani means 'misery', and local tradition confirms that it was built after Sundiata's flight there. Mandingos do not rebuild ruined towns, for they believe that this is to invite a repetition of the tragedy which ruined them in the first place. They move to a new site nearby to keep watch over the spirits of their ancestors.

So we can conclude that at least one of the sites of Mali's capital was about 250 miles south of Koumbi Saleh, site of the capital of the Empire of Ghana, which it overthrew. Mali was much more extensive than Ghana. At one time much of modern Guinea, Senegal, Sudan and modern Ghana was subject to the Emperor whose capital Ibn Batuta tells us was ten miles from the Sankara river. Other important towns in this broad domain were Taghaza, Walata, Karsakhun and, further downstream on the Niger, Timbuktu and Gao, which was later to become the capital of the Empire of the Songhai, which overcame Mali. Then there were Muli, the modern Muri, near Niamey, which was the eastern frontier town of Mali, and Yufi. The latter was probably in the area of the modern Nupe between Jebba and Lokoja, and is described as one of the largest of negro towns in the fourteenth century, ruled over by a powerful chief who had placed it out of bounds to all non-negroes.

The Empire of Mali seems to have been even wealthier than that of Ghana. The media of exchange were salt and cowrie shells. The salt was worth 20 to 30 mithqals a camel-load (two blocks) in the capital in normal times, and 40 when there was a shortage. At Walata, nearer to its source, the salt could be bought for 8 to 10 mithqals a camel-load. 1,150 cowrie shells were exchanged for a gold dinar in the fourteenth century in Mali.

The wealth of the Emperor was based on the trade in gold across the desert. And this wealth was indeed fabulous. Mansa Kankan Musa,[2] took 60,000 men to Mecca and eighty camels each bearing 300 lb. of gold, together with 500 slaves each carrying a golden staff weighing 500 mithqals. Small wonder that Cairo gaped! The famous gold nugget to which you remember the Emperor of Ghana had tethered his horse was now in the imperial treasury at Mali. Gold was obtained from Wangara, and was taken to the capital and other large towns to be exchanged for the salt and other goods brought by the Arabs across the desert. Sometimes the people of Mali would themselves venture into the desert town of Taghaza to buy salt with their gold.

Taghaza was a rather unattractive town, we read, whose houses were built of blocks of salt, and roofed with camel skins. But it had the vital commodity which the people of Mali needed and could pay well for. So slaves of the negro Massufa

---

[1] P. 28.
[2] P.36

tribe lived more or less permanently at Taghaza, digging for salt for their Berber masters. These slaves lived on the excellent dates which the Arab traders brought them from Sijilmasa, and also on camels' flesh and millet - quite a good diet for slaves anywhere!

Another indication of the wealth of fourteenth-century Mali was the highly organized nature of the trade across the desert. Although, as you can imagine, the journey was dangerous and unpleasant, there was so much coming and going of merchants to and from the capital that something almost like an entire tourist agency had developed, complete with guides. On leaving Taghaza, with its brackish water, and its flies, a caravan would set out on the ten-day journey to Tasarahla. The next stop would be Walata, which was the northernmost outpost of the Empire. From here a takshif (guide) would set out to meet the party four nights out, and lead them into the town. In Walata in lbn Batuta's day, the Emperor had a Farba or Governor who sat on a carpet under an arch, with guards carrying lances and bows in front of him, and Massufa headmen behind. The Farba would only speak to strangers through an interpreter, just like a modern West African chief. The food here was good, with water-melon in the shade of the date palms, plenty of mutton, and a good underground water supply. And the people could afford Egyptian cotton.

From Walata the traveller to the capital of Mali found that he need only carry salt, glass ornaments, and spices, in order to be able to barter for his daily needs. The variety of food increased — there was now chicken, pulped lotus fruit, rice, funi (kuskus), haricot beans, and hippopotamus meat cut from animals caught with harpoons. And once in the capital itself, we find descriptions of tremendous wealth. The Emperor's armour bearers had gold and silver quivers, swords ornamented with gold and carried in golden scabbards, and they bore gold and silver lances and crystal maces. But even the ordinary people seem to have been well off. Some of the houses had candles not common commodities even in Europe in those days.

The women of Mali are described by Arab travellers as beautiful, and given more respect than the men. Lines of inheritance here, as in ancient Ghana, passed through the female line. Although many of them were zealous Muslims, they did not wear veils. Like typical Muslim women elsewhere, however, they never travelled with their husbands. If in Walata they could afford cotton cloth, in the capital the women had a range of even more expensive fabrics available to them - silks, and a 'velvety red tunic' out of which the coverings for the Emperor's 'bembi' (platform) were made. There was also, however, quite a lot of local weaving done; although perhaps some of it, like the 'kente' weaving in modern Ghana, was done with imported thread.

We have already noted[1] the Massufa slaves in Taghaza; and in the capital itself there were many more slaves. Your social position was measured by the number of slaves and maidservants you had. But all inhabitants, bond or free, were submissive to their Emperor. They swore by his name, and anyone summoned to an audience with him would put on his oldest clothes, and a skull-cap in place of his usual turban. He would raise his clothes and trousers knee-high, and move forward towards the Emperor in an attitude of great respect, hitting the ground with his elbows. He would then listen with bent back to the Emperor on the raised 'bembi'. If His Majesty saw fit to reply to his petition, his humble subject would uncover his back and throw dust over himself, rather like a chicken. On such occasions many of the petitioners would recount their acts of service and devotion to the Emperor. Those standing around would twang their bow strings as a sign of acclaim for the narrator's words.

These audiences were obviously important social occasions, as well as ceremonial occasions. The 'bembi' was in an open square, and the general public would shelter in the shade of the trees to watch the show, whilst the Emperor had his silk canopy surmounted by a golden bird to protect him from the hot sun. We read of magnificent bows and quivers, and gold and silver two-stringed guitars, in the Emperor's retinue. There were also trumpets, drums and bugles, which would sound out to herald his arrival and departure. Two horses and two goats always stood near at hand to protect the assembled company from evil spirits. A special place would be reserved for the emirs, who were probably subject kings, and one of whose duties was to keep the flies off the imperial 'bembi'. Also in attendance on these splendid occasions were the Emperor's military commanders, chaplain, interpreter, wives, and slave girls with gold and silver fillets through their hair. The linguist or 'Dugha' would play an instrument with small calabashes at its lower end, which must have resembled the 'balangie' still in use in Sierra Leone today. The Dugha's duties were to chant poems of praise to the Emperor for his victories and his other deeds of valour. The women and girls would also sing, and play their instruments. Thirty youths, dressed in red woollen tunics and white skull caps would accompany the girls' singing, beating drums slung from their shoulders. Finally, boys would turn cart-wheels and do nimble acrobatic exercises, and give displays of swordsmanship.

On feast days there was the extra treat of poets, wearing feathers and wooden heads with red beaks, who would recite poems encouraging their Emperor to follow the noble example of his predecessors. Then the chief poet would stand on the steps leading up to the 'bembi', lay his head on the Emperor's lap, mount to the 'bembi' itself, and then lay his head first on the right imperial shoulder then on the left imperial shoulder - a custom we are told was older in Mali than Mohammedanism.

---

[1] P. 38

The Empire of Mali

But just as behind all the pomp and ceremony there lay the military skill to conquer Gao, so also there lay an efficient administrative system for running the internal affairs of the Empire. You could not enter Mali, for example, unless your papers were in order. Ibn Batuta had to write ahead to the semi-permanent non-negro residents of Mali to ask them to get these papers ready for him. He says that otherwise he would have had difficulty in crossing the Sankara River into the capital itself. But neither military skill nor good administrators can have much effect under a bad Emperor. The Mali Emperor during Ibn Batuta's visit was Sulayman, who died in 1359. He was also the last of the able Emperors, and his death plunged the Empire into civil war. Sulayman's son Kamba was slain in a long struggle with a grandson of Mansa Kankan Musa, who became in turn Mansa Mari Jata II. The latter was a cruel and selfish ruler, who even sold the famous gold nugget the Emperor of Mali had won from the Emperor of Ghana. No doubt, therefore, Man Jata II's subjects were glad when sleeping sickness cut short his life. Musa II, his son and successor, was rather weak and his very able Prime Minister Jata had to struggle hard to keep the crumbling Empire together. Whilst Jata was suppressing a revolt by the Sultan of Bornu in the east, Timbuktu in the north was captured by Tuareg desert tribes. The Fulani were also on the attack.[1] Then the Songhai of Gao rebelled, and it was they who finally replaced Mali in about 1475 as the most important state in West Africa.[2]

---

[1] P.56
[2] P. 49

5

The Empire of the Songhai

Every country has ancient monuments of one sort or another - old buildings and objects of historical interest. It used to be believed once that the only such buildings and objects still surviving in West Africa were those dating from the period when the people of Europe held political and economic power over the people of West Africa. There are, of course, still many fascinating historical relics dating from this period — the old slave factory on Bunce Island in Sierra Leone (see map page 86), and the string of forts and castles dotting the Ghana coast are very good examples.

But there are some less well-known buildings in West Africa which date from an even earlier period, a period when West African civilization was at its height in the Empires of Ghana, Mali, and the Songhai. One such building is the great mosque of Sankore at Timbuktu, which provided a very famous centre of learning and religion during the fifteenth century and later. It is for the most part a low, sprawling building, with a conical prickly-looking structure, rather like a miniature pyramid, dominating the rest of the building. This structure no doubt provided a vantage point from which the faithful could be called to prayer, and watch could be kept for approaching enemies.

Further downstream, just round the sweeping northern bend of the Niger, is another ancient monument that deserves to be much better known than it is, and which, like the Sankore mosque, I hope you will be able to visit some day. It is the tomb of the Askias, Emperors of the Songhai people; and it is to be found at Gao or Gaw-Gaw, their ancient capital. This tomb is a massive, rather unattractive, but compact building, set, like the mosque at Timbuktu, in semi-desert country, which is clothed only in scrubby grass and low trees. This once proud city, mistress of a vast domain, is today little more than the market and meeting ground of nomadic and semi-nomadic tribes, and a convenient ford. The only feature of the landscape that has remained unchanged for the past thousand years is the camel, still kneeling obediently to let his master mount and dismount, still loping along with his ungainly stride.

But at least we do know the approximate boundaries of *this* Empire, and the precise situation of its capital. So we have been able to discover quite a lot about it and its rulers. The Songhai people probably came originally from the area where the Rivers Rima and Niger meet. The eastern boundaries of their Empire stretched, at their most extensive, as far as Bussa in the south, and Kano in the north. And Gao you will find clearly marked on most modern maps of West Africa, for a busy town still exists there today.

The Songhai did not choose this particular spot for their capital by chance. You will remember how in our second chapter[1] I remarked on the importance of easy communications and fertile soil if human civilization is to develop in any part of the world. History teaches us clearly that a primitive man is not an inferior man, but an isolated one; and that civilized man is not a superior one, but an accessible one. In the middle Niger, as in the Euphrates and Nile, we have an

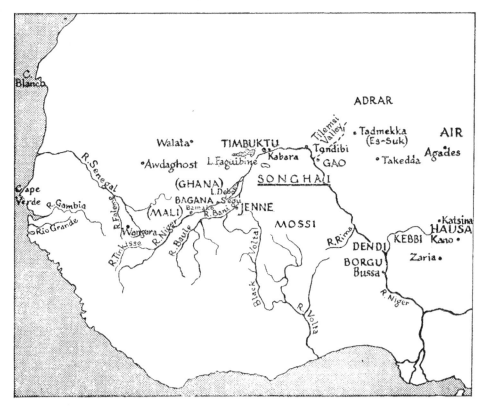

Map 5 The Empire of the Songhai (about A.D. 690 to A.D. 1591).

---

[1] P. 21

excellent example of fertile land giving the people living on it both the leisure and the contacts (with other peoples also attracted by the soil's fertility) which are necessary for progress.

If you find Bamako and Bussa on the Niger, and look at the stretch of river between them, you will be looking at a thousand miles of waterway which is uninterrupted by falls or rapids. The riverbanks are lined by a water grass called borgu which cattle love, and by the fan palm tree, whose trunk makes such excellent canoes. At both ends of this peaceful pasturage there are rapids which help to make it easily defended against undesirable visitors, and along its whole length there are picturesque islands and inlets.

It is not surprising, therefore, that this stretch of the Niger should have been at one time or another the home of some of the most energetic and well-organized tribes in West Africa. It was a very desirable piece of country, and only the strongest of tribes could make it its own for any great length of time. And the strongest tribe of all seized the most desirable spot of all, where the long Tilemsi valley carrying a trade route from North Africa south-westwards across the Sahara reached the Niger.

It was here on the northern bank of the Niger, at Gao, one of the most important cross-roads of West Africa, that the negro Songhai had settled about the seventh century. They had come upstream from the Dendi and Bussa areas, and, in spite of frequent wars against the desert Berber tribes, they had multiplied rapidly. They soon occupied the whole of the lower half of the coveted thousand-mile stretch, and some of their descendants live there today.

But unfortunately this virile tribe split into two rival groups: the Sorko, who were mainly fishermen, and the Gabibi, who were mainly farmers. In such a war the fishermen were naturally at a great advantage, being so much more mobile than the farmers. But the fishermen met their match at the hands of the much better-armed Berber Lemta tribe from the desert to the north, whose chief, Za Aliamen, conquered them in about 700. He forced both the farmers and the fishermen to recognize him as their ruler. So it was that the royal family of the Songhai Emperors who used the name 'Za' was founded. A long line of Za Emperors was to follow Aliamen, before the royal house was overthrown by the Mali Emperor Kankan Musa's general in 1325, as we have seen.[1]

The Songhai were in the eighth century a completely pagan tribe, of course; for Islam had not yet reached West Africa. When it did, 300 years later, it was through the Lemta Tuareg that the Songhai received the new faith. The Za line of Emperors was still ruling but was now, through frequent intermarriage, at least partly negro. The Lemta living in the Empire were now its subjects, not its rulers. And as so often happens, the subjects lent many of their customs to their rulers, and more and more of the upper class Songhai were adopting Islam. Gao itself

---

[1] P. 36

was divided, like Koumbi in ancient Ghana, into a Muslim and a pagan section. The former was inhabited mainly by merchants.

In 1009 there was an important event. The Songhai Emperor himself, Za Kosoi, became a Muslim - probably the first negro Emperor to do so. You know what a powerful example the decision of a ruler in a matter like this can be. The conversion of the Songhai to Islam was now even more rapid than before. All Za Kosoi's successors were Muslims. One of them, Za Yosiboi, last of the Za line, had the misfortune to be on the throne when Kankan Musa's army attacked Gao in 1325; but as far as the Empire's religious life was concerned this defeat brought its advantages. Musa, calling there on his way back from his famous hadj, built a fine new mosque, and a beautiful palace, in Gao; the architect was a Spanish poet called Es-Saheli who was a member of the Mali Emperor's retinue. And the Songhai rulers paid more than the mere price of defeat for their new mosque : Musa took Za Yosiboi's two sons back to his capital with him; and for fifty years (1325 - 75) the Songhai remained a subject people of Mali.

Nineteen emperors of the Sonni line followed the thirty-one Zas on the Songhai throne. They too were Mohammedans, although some of them, like Sonni Ali (the last but one and in many ways the greatest of the Sonnis) were not very sincere in practising their faith. We learn how Ali would not take the trouble to say the five daily prayers at their appointed time. Instead he would repeat them all together in the evening, and, when he felt particularly lazy, would merely recite the names of the prayers. And he secretly practised pagan rites at the same time.

The line of Sonni was followed by that of Askia Mohamed I, Askia the Great, who was Sonni Ali's Prime Minister under the name Mohamed Abubaker El-Touri. He really was a devout Muslim, who believed that he had been sent by God to replace on the throne a family that was not. On his return from his hadj he was created 'Sarkin Musulmi', or spiritual ruler of all Muslims in West Africa, by the Khalif of Cairo. We still use the term 'Zarikin' for the head of the Muslims in a particular town. There were to be eleven Askia emperors.

Songhai's greatest power was won during the fifteenth and sixteenth centuries. Gao was by then a very important market. There were other important markets in the Songhai Empire by the sixteenth century. Two hundred and fifty miles away up the Tilemsi valley was Tadmekka, or Es-Suk, an even older town, whose ruins can still be seen today. Es-Suk is the Arab term for 'The Market', and it exchanged trade between the West African towns of Gao and Timbuktu, and the North African towns of Kairwan and Ghadames.

You should now be able to draw on a map of your own the two great parallel trade routes which provided such important commercial life-lines for our ancestors before their attention was diverted by the arrival of sea-borne European traders. The first, the westerly one, you will remember[1] started at Sijilmasa in what is now Morocco, and ran through Taghaza and Walata to Awdaghost and Koumbi. The easterly one is the one passing through Es-Suk and Gao, which I have just described. The nature of the goods travelling along these two routes was probably very similar, but the volume of trade along the western route reached its peak much earlier than that along the eastern route.

Another important Songhai town formed, with Gao and Es-Suk. an almost perfect isosceles triangle. This was Takedda, directly to the east of Gao. Here was an ideal triangle of trade: Gao, the agricultural and fishing centre; Es-Suk, the market; and Takedda, the industrial, copper-mining town. Each depended on the others, contributing to the constant flow of goods and currency on which any nation's health depends. We hear that as early as the eleventh century gold was being used in Es-Suk as coinage; but it was plain, unstamped gold, not minted into actual coins.

The city which ranked second to Gao in importance in Songhai was to the west - Timbuktu, not much more than 200 miles away as the crow flies, but much further if you followed the winding northern sweep of the mighty river. With both the eastern and the western trade routes you have drawn within easy reach of it, Timbuktu can be said to have remained for several centuries the commercial capital of West Africa. Here the salt from Taghaza, the gold dust from Jenne and Wangara, and the fish from Kabara (Timbuktu's little port) changed hands, and wealth multiplied. The original tents of Timbuktu soon gave way to huts; and although it was Es-Saheli's mosque in Gao which first used burnt bricks, Timbuktu soon started to use this new building material too. The foundations of these original brick buildings may be seen in both towns today; and there are brick buildings of similar style standing in Timbuktu now.

The Songhai rulers were hardly less wealthy, at the height of their power, than the Mali. One hundred and seventy years after Musa's hadj,[2] in 1494, Askia Mohamed I set out to show that he was a match for Musa both in devotion to Allah and in possession of riches. Askia took on *his* hadj a caravan of 500 cavalry, 1,000 infantry, and a fortune of 300,000 pieces of gold, two-thirds of which were to be used to meet expenses, and the rest as gifts. By this time indeed, most of Europe's gold came from West Africa.

Another clear lesson to be learnt from the history of the Western Sudan at this time is that religion, trade and learning tend to move along the same routes. Here, the trader's ledger, the imam's Koran, and the scholar's scrolls were never very far apart from each other. We have noted how the capital of ancient Ghana, Koumbi, had attracted many scholars and merchants. Amongst the finest of the scholars were a people from Adrar, deep in the desert. These people were called

---

[1] P. 28
[2] p. 38

the Jedala, and they had sharp, inquiring minds, and a deep love of learning. When Koumbi fell to the Susu in 1203[1] the Jedala, fearing perhaps that the interests of the music- and dance-loving Susu were very different from their own, joined the many refugees who left Koumbi to found a new settlement at Walata, 100 miles to the north-west. This now became for a time the new 'Athens of West Africa'. It was later succeeded by Timbuktu, when the growing commercial importance of the latter in turn attracted to it the Jedala, who were traders as well as scholars. It was at Timbuktu that the great university and mosque of Sankore were established, to which men of letters came from far beyond the coasts of Africa. It was essentially a Muslim university, with great historians such as Ahmed Baba and architects and poets such as Es-Saheli (whom we have already met)[2] working there. But it was also a truly African university. Arabic was the social *lingua franca*, but Songhai seems to have been used as the medium of teaching and research. Degrees were awarded to the best students, and we know that the academic standards reached were at least as high as those of the better-known North African universities. In fact we read of one scholar from one of the latter institutions who came to Timbuktu hoping to be appointed a lecturer, and decided to stay there as a student.

And so the spread of learning in West Africa continued - Koumbi, Walata, Timbuktu, and finally during the pre-European period, Jenne. The spread has of course continued in more recent times - Fourah Bay, Achimota, Ibadan, Legon. But let us for the time being go back to Jenne. This was perhaps the safest refuge for West African scholars of its day, though not the most famous. It was the city situated furthest up the Niger basin of all the great cities in that basin, and was much more easily defended than Timbuktu, for example. Jenne could only be reached along narrow streams and canals, which often wound through treacherous swamps. The Soninke had founded this town in the thirteenth century, and for the next 500 years more and more scholars, both from North and West Africa, made their homes here. In fact according to Es-Sadi, himself a native of Timbuktu, the development of the latter town was due to the fact that so many caravans bound for Jenne had to pass through it. A university was founded at Jenne, and medicine was taught. We hear of difficult surgical operations being performed there, so there must have been something in the nature of a teaching hospital.

The people of Jenne were very proud of their culture, and determined to make full use of the natural advantages of situation and terrain in defending it. So when the all-conquering Songhai ruler Sonni Ali tried to subdue it, he found he had taken on the most difficult task of his career: a task which, it is said, defeated many kings of Mali.

---

[1] P. 32
[2] P. 45

The two princes whom Mansa Kankan Musa took home with him to Mali[1] from Gao in 1325 succeeded in escaping eventually, and in 1375 they freed their city from the weakening rule of Mali. Each became in turn Emperor of the Songhai, and they are honoured today as the founders of the Sonni line of emperors. For the next century Gao waited patiently for an opportunity to win back from Mali the great metropolis of Timbuktu as well. Its chance came when the desert Tuaregs captured Timbuktu, cleared it of Mandingos, and appointed a governor there. This governor soon became dissatisfied with his small share of the booty, and so invited Sonni Ali, who had become Emperor of the Songhai in 1466, to enter the city. The size of the approaching Songhai army frightened even the governor who had called it in, however, and every Tuareg fled from Timbuktu. All Sonni Ali had to do that day in January 1468 was to march downstream to the nearest bridge, cross, and march back upstream into Timbuktu.

Sonni Ali was a very cruel man. Although he had recaptured Timbuktu for the Songhai without losing a drop of blood, he decided to teach the people of the city never again to accept so easily the rule of foreigners, whether they were Mandingos of Mali or Tuaregs from the desert. He slew many of the good folk of Timbuktu, and created for himself a very evil reputation. It is particularly difficult to excuse his action when we remember that Timbuktu was not the easiest of towns to defend, and that the Tuareg were very fierce and skilful fighters.

As had been the case with the Empire of Ghana between 1076 and 1088,[2] the Empire of the Songhai still had at that time a royal family which was at least partly of Berber origin, although most of the people themselves were negroes. Many of the citizens of Timbuktu itself were, however, also partly Berber, owing to the long trading links they had with North Africa. So Sonni Ali's harshness is all the more difficult to understand. In any case he now turned his attention to Jenne, to which town and to Walata, many of the Timbuktu scholars from Sankore had fled in terror at the news of his approach. But as we have seen,[3] Jenne was much more difficult to attack successfully than Timbuktu. Not only was the terrain more difficult, but this time there was no treacherous governor to invite the enemy in.

Sonni Ali soon gave up the idea of making an open attack on the famous university and market town, and settled down to starve it into surrender. This took seven years, seven months, and seven days; and both besiegers and besieged decided to give up at about the same time. We should expect the Songhai Emperor to deal even more cruelly with Jenne than with Timbuktu, for giving

---

[1] P. 45
[2] P. 31
[3] P. 47

him so much trouble. But perhaps his men were too exhausted even to massacre and burn. Or was Sonni Ali simply an older and wiser man? At all events he was the soul of kindness to all, and even married the mother of the young king of Jenne as if to prove that there were no ill feelings. It is now, about 1475,[1] that we can say that the Songhai Empire replaced Mali as the most powerful state in West Africa.

One good result of all this was that the scholars were once more able to return to their books and experiments. Sonni Ali wanted not to destroy Mansa Kankan Musa's vast Empire but to inherit it intact. So he increased his own power and prestige by defeating Mali's enemies, such as the Tuareg and the Fulani, one by one. In this atmosphere of relative peace and quiet at home, Timbuktu was able to welcome back some of her Jedala scholars[2] and their disciples. It is amusing to read in the *Tarikh es Sudan* (History of the Sudan), the great work written in Arabic two centuries later by Es-Sadi, the half-Hausa, half-Fulani Timbuktu historian, of the change their exile in Walata had brought about in these scholars. Previously they had rather snobbishly forbidden their children to join in the games of the less fortunate children of the Timbuktu streets. As a result the learned Jedala families had grown up weak and sickly, and when it came to fleeing before Sonni Ali 'bearded men were trembling with fright at having to mount a camel, and falling off again when the animal got up'. Having learnt that over-protection of children can do harm, when they eventually returned home the Jedala allowed their children much more freedom to play as they wished.

Sonni Ali came up against only one enemy that he was unable to crush - the Mossi of Yatenga. We shall learn more about them in a later volume. They did not directly affect the fortunes of the Songhai Empire. They may have helped, however, to put Sonni Ali in a bad temper again; for when he next visited Timbuktu, towards the end of his life, he once more ill treated its people. There was another, though probably smaller, flight of scholars and merchants from the city. In 1492, whilst returning to Gao from a campaign against the Fulani, Sonni was halfway across a small stream when a wall of water swept down on him without warning, and he was drowned. People said, of course, that this was a punishment for all his cruelty.

His son was succeeded in 1493 by Sonni's Prime Minister who, as I have mentioned,[3] founded the Askia line of Songhai Emperors after having seized power in a *coup d'etat*. The Askia line lasted for almost exactly a century; for it was on April 12, 1591, that the Moors were to destroy their Empire. The first Askia was undoubtedly the greatest. Unlike the old line, this was a pure negro line, of the Soninke tribe. Askia I, who ruled until 1529, brought the power of the

---

[1] P. 41
[2] P. 46
[3] P.45

49

Songhai to a height they had never before reached. The administration of the Empire was centralized, learning and religion were given their proper place, and a peaceful and orderly atmosphere allowed them to thrive.

Askia's hadj has already[1] given us proof of his tremendous wealth; but as well as being a very spiritually minded man, Askia was a scholarly and generous one. The historian Leo Africanus tells us how in Timbuktu in this reign there were 'many judges, doctors and priests, all receiving salaries from the king. He pays great respect to men of learning. There is a big demand for books in manuscript. . . . More profit is made from the book trade than from any other line of business.' So you see bookshops crowded with customers are nothing new in West Africa! But commerce generally flourished in the Empire of Askia the Great owing to the skilful way in which he built up an efficient central government.

He used this wealth to fight many wars on his borders, but they were as much wars of religion as of expansion. He sought to convert to Islam the pagan tribes to the west and south which had previously been ruled by Mali. Under him the Songhai Empire was extended until it stretched from Segu in the west to Air in the north-east, and so was almost as extensive as Mali at its height.[2] Still not content, however, Askia decided to launch an attack in a completely new direction - against the Hausa states.

Our next chapter will tell us more about these. Now we need only note how little resistance they offered to Askia. Only Kano, of all the walled towns round which these states clustered, was able to hold Askia off for any time. But Songhai Emperors had no respect for a weak enemy, and it was the rulers of Katsina and Zaria who were slain by Askia, whilst the ruler of Kano, having surrendered after a hard year's siege, retained his throne, and was given in marriage one of Askia's own daughters! He was, however, required to sign a treaty agreeing to send one-third of all taxes to Gao, and not to rebel.

So the Empire of the Songhai grew eastwards as well as southwards and westwards. Now Askia turned north, to try to put an end to the constant invasion of his borders by the Tuareg. From the newly conquered Hausa states he was able to move against the most important of the Tuareg bases, Agades, in the region of Air, immediately to the north. Having conquered this town, his Empire now reached Lake Chad in the east and the Atlantic in the west. Only the coastal forests, where the horses on which the Songhai depended were killed by the tsetse fly, were now beyond his conquering reach.

In this huge domain lived now a community whose way of life was orderly, happy, and prosperous, thanks to their Emperor's skill and wisdom. We read of the careful standardization of weights and measures, for example, and of the creation of an army of professional soldiers to replace the motley band of farm

[1] P.46
[2] P.38

recruits whose crops had formerly spoiled in the sun whilst they fought clumsily and sullenly. Askia's own sons were sent to the Timbuktu university of Sankore. But Gao itself attracted many great scholars. One of them was El Maghili, a North African who advised Askia on how to improve his government, and persuaded him to persecute the Jews. The latter were now coming to Songhai in increasing numbers - a sure sign of its prosperity.

And so Askia the Great drew to the end of a very prosperous reign. He still had to face many difficulties before it finally ended. First Kanta, King of Kebbi (one of the Hausa states we are to study in the next chapter) rebelled successfully against him. Surame, Kanta's capital, was so secure behind its seven stone walls that Kanta and his successors henceforth maintained their independence not only from the Songhai, but also from Bornu and Sokoto.

However, in 1528 Askia's eldest son persuaded two of his brothers to join him in a rebellion against their father. The following year the great ruler was overthrown, and abdicated; and three years later he went into exile on an unhealthy Niger island when the Songhai army took control of the government. The old ex-Emperor was now almost ninety; but perhaps these rather sad closing years of his life were cheered by one bright item of news. When he had conquered the Tuareg in Agades many years before,[1] Askia had cleared the town of Berbers, and planted in it a community of Songhai. This small and isolated community has frequently been attacked by Berbers since, and many of its members have inter-married with non-negroes. But the settlement succeeded in beating off all attackers. Askia was able to follow its fortunes with great satisfaction from his exile; and, since it still survives today, this little negro colony in Berber territory provides an opportunity, particularly to pupils in Northern Nigeria, to visit a living memorial to a great ruler.

The army commander who sent Askia into exile was a bad soldier as well as a bad man. The rebellious Kanta of Kebbi put the whole Songhai army to flight when that army attacked him; and this defeat led to the overthrow of army rule in Gao, and the return of Askia to his old palace. Here he died in 1538 in surroundings fit for an emperor.

Three sons of Askia followed each other on the throne, and their reigns were to hasten the end of the Empire. For a war now developed between the Songhai rulers and the Sultan of Morocco over the salt mines of Taghaza - Ibn Batuta's 'unattractive village'.[2] Although near the borders of Morocco, these mines were claimed as Songhai property. The Sultan of Morocco knew, however, that whoever controlled Taghaza controlled the rich West African trade. Benefiting from the internal struggles in Gao which I have described, he seized Taghaza in 1585 and sent army after army against Gao itself. The Songhai might have

---

[1] P. 50
[2] P. 38

withstood these attacks for a long time; but revolts by the Hausa state of Katsina had further weakened Songhai military power, and the skilled leadership of Askia was no longer available. Most important of all, the Moroccans had European firearms, which the Songhai did not. As we are to see, if the Muslim trader came to us across the desert on a camel, the Christian trader came to us over the sea behind a gun. At the battle of Tondibi a link between the two appeared for the first time. This battle was fought fifty miles from Gao, on April 12, 1591. A Spaniard called Djouder Pasha (or Judar Pasha), the Sultan of Morocco's Spanish general, completely routed the Songhai army by using 2,500 muskets against bows, arrows, spears, swords, and a herd of stampeding cattle. He then went on to capture Gao and Timbuktu; and although this campaign cost the Moors 3,000 men, they took great loot back to Marrakesh. In their main object, however, they failed; for they never discovered the source of Songhai's gold. In 1618 the Sultan decided that to retain his hold on Songhai was more trouble than it was worth, and withdrew his men. By then, however, although Songhai leaders had arisen from time to time to shout defiance at the Moors, their Empire, once so powerful, was crumbling under the corrupt and incompetent rule of its foreign conquerors.

6

The Bornu and Hausa States

(see Map 6: The Bornu and Hausa States)

L ake Chad is right in the north-eastern corner of the area we call West Africa, and close to its western shores there developed from about the eighth century onwards an important group of states speaking a common language, Hausa. The Hausa language is spoken by more of us in West Africa than is any other language, European or African. It is no longer the language of any particular tribe, although it must have been so once. It has spread partly because the people who spoke it originally seem to have been energetic travellers and traders, and partly because it has recently come to be used more and more as the common language of West African Muslims. It is curious to read, therefore, that one of the reasons why these Hausa states were conquered by the Fulani at the beginning of the nineteenth century[1] was that their people were not at that time regarded by the zealous Fulani as good enough Muslims!

On those western shores, as in most other parts of West Africa, negro and non-negro people have lived for at least a thousand years in peace and friendship. The non-negroes are Tuareg (nomadic Berbers), and in the tenth century were from the Lemta tribe. In addition to the negro and non-negro residents, there were at that time 'strangers' in the area, merchants who were not permanently settled there, but stayed only as long as necessary to complete their business, returning afterwards to their North African homes. These birds of passage were known as the Wasuri by the people of the largest of the Hausa states, Bornu.

The ruling family in Bornu at the end of the ninth century A.D. came from the Berber residents, as seems to have been the case at one time or another in nearly

---

[1] P. 56

all the great West African states. This family was called Sefuwa, after Sef, its founder; and the capital was originally at Njimi, of which the exact position has unfortunately not yet been traced. The Sefuwa rulers gradually extended their authority round the shores of the lake, and then spread westwards. A group of their subjects called the Zaghawa, also Berbers, ranged far to the west, settling in negro communities and inter-marrying with them - something the Lemta had never done in the region north and east of the lake.

Thus it was that the state of Bornu developed in about the eighth century. Since Njimi is in the region called Kanem, the latter was the name by which the state first became known. It had a mixed population which was both adventurous and energetic. Still further west, a process similar to that I have just described led to the formation of seven much smaller Hausa states. These were known as the Hausa Bokwoi; and their names were Daura, Kano, Zaria, Gobir, Katsina, Rano and Biram.

Rivalry soon arose amongst the eight states, and there were many wars. We do not know much about these wars; but Bornu was more successful than the others in enlarging her boundaries at her neighbours' expense. Bornu was to survive as a sovereign state until the seventeenth century; and its long life, like that of Ghana,[1] was at least partly due to her having many craftsmen in iron. Bornu also had a well-developed feudal system. The ruler had an executive council called the 'Great Council' of twelve. At first the members of this Council were usually members of his family, and completely under his control. Later, the king's advisers fought each other for power, and helped ultimately to destroy the king's power too.

As time passed, Bornu tended to have much more contact with North Africa than with other parts of West Africa, whilst the opposite was the case with the states of the Hausa Bokwoi. The trade route across the desert to Bornu ran through Tripoli, the Fezzan, and Kawar.[2] Bornu was a famous horse market; like Gao, it also bought copper, from Takedda.

Then towards the end of the eleventh century, Islam reached Lake Chad. Both the people of Bornu and those of the Hausa Bokwoi proved ready converts. The process of extending the borders of Bornu went on side by side with the spread of Islam in the whole of the Lake Chad area, and was closely connected with it. Two twelfth-century rulers of Bornu, Durama and Selma, strengthened the state greatly, as did a fifteenth-century ruler, Mai Ali Ghajideni. Mai founded a new capital at Birni after a heavy defeat at the hands of Kanta of Kebbi, whom you will remember as a rebel subject of Askia the Great of Songhai.[3] Mai's successor Idris II showed, however, that the people of Bornu had no intention of

---

[1] P.27
[2] P. 11
[3] P. 51

54

abandoning Njimi and Kanem. He defeated the Bulala, a tribe of Berbers who claimed Kanem, and brought it once more under the control of Bornu.

It was Idris' successor Mohamed V who brought the state to its greatest strength. Secure on all her frontiers, with a thriving trade across the desert, and a firmly established state religion, Bornu, though smaller than the other states we have studied, was a very good example of a well-ordered nation. And when, as happened in the seventeenth century, her rulers gave assistance to some of their subject Tuareg tribes in frontier wars against the latter's enemies, even areas as far away as Air fell under Bornu's control. Agades, which we have seen[1] was one of Askia the Great's most important desert conquests, and an important market, was in Air. It controlled yet another trade route, linking the Hausa states with North Africa through Ghadames and Ghat. In addition to having its own route, Bornu could and did now throttle or divert the trade of the states of the Hausa Bokwoi.

You may like to add this route to those already on your map. But as you do so remember that no map can show you all the channels of trade across the desert. There must have been a whole web of feeder routes and cross-routes linking the main ones I have described. But the latter did undoubtedly carry the great bulk of commerce between North and West Africa.

The very weakness of the Hausa Bokwoi states, however, for which Bornu was partly responsible,[2] was eventually to prove a danger to Bornu herself. Those seven states had taken their names from their capitals. These were for the most part relatively small walled cities which remain today much as they were three or four hundred years ago. The outer walls of Kano are 30 to 50 feet high, and 11 miles long. They form, with the inner walls, formidable obstacles to any attacker. The defence tactics used by the people of the countryside was a very simple one. At the first sign of danger, they would flee into the capital and barricade themselves in. In this arid country the only reliable source of water was inside the walls, and sooner or later the besiegers would be forced by thirst to abandon the siege.

This meant, however, that the Hausa Bokwoi were always on the defensive. They did, behind the safety of their walls, develop efficient systems of government. Each state had its king, who appointed ministers, judges, and a civil service. Seven more Hausa states developed in and after the sixteenth century, and these were modelled on the Hausa Bokwoi. They are known as the Banza Bokwoi or 'upstart states', and their names are Kebbi,[3] Zamfara, Nupe, Gwari, Yauri, Kororofa, and Ilorin.

---

[1] P. 50
[2] P. 54
[3] P.51

Through all fourteen Hausa states Islam spread even more rapidly than it had done elsewhere in West Africa. This was particularly true after the fourteenth century, when Mali imams launched a missionary campaign in Hausa country, at the invitation of Yagi, King of Kano.

But, disunited, fighting often amongst themselves, and content with keeping their boundaries narrow and well defined, the Hausa-speaking people were never empire builders. Their importance in West Africa is really commercial. Gobir, for example, bought Takedda copper in exchange for rice, and in all the states expert leather and metal workers were to be found. Their way of life, at first distinctly Berber, became more and more negro, and spread, with the trade which their people sought, all over West Africa. Their language was written in modified Arabic characters,[1] and so spread far quicker than any other West African language.

The Hausa-speaking people helped to spread more than trade and Islam. Their system of law and administration, although practised on a relatively small scale in their own states, was regarded as a model by many much larger ones. The courts of the rulers of Katsina and Daura in particular were visited by many students of these subjects.

Thus whilst Hausa culture, so widely spread, is not likely soon to disappear, the Hausa states themselves, militarily weak, were in constant danger. Even Bornu was being attacked by the beginning of the sixteenth century. Kanta of Kebbi, who had broken away from the Songhai,[2] had already repulsed an attack by Mai Ali of Bornu on Surame, Kanta's capital. But a far cleverer enemy was on the way - the Fulani.

The Fulani, as we shall see, are not negroes. They had once been among the subjects of the Empire of Ghana and, on its fall, they moved westwards to Tekrur near the coast. From then on they were constantly on the move. Some of them, the Gidda, settled in towns, inter-married with negroes, and accepted Islam. But the majority remained cow-keepers, keeping themselves completely separate. These pastoral Fulani, called Boroje, are light-skinned, and their features generally clearly show their non-negro origin. They remain largely pagan, and have set up their own states, such as Futa Jallon in what is today Guinea. We find them nibbling at the borders of Mali towards the end of the fifteenth century.[3]

But it was the more aggressive Gidda Fulani who reached Hausaland and Bornu, settling there from about 1450 onwards in increasing numbers. They mixed very well with the Hausa, and there was in the Hausa towns an almost complete blend of negro and non-negro, except that the metal and leather craftsmen remain to this day purely non-negro. The Fulani, in fact, learnt the

---

[1] P. 21

[2] P. 51

[3] P. 41

lessons of Islam so well from the Hausas that they were soon pointing accusing fingers at their teachers for not being zealous in the faith. At the beginning of the nineteenth century Usuman dan Fodio, a Fulani preacher of what he considered the purest form of Islam, declared a jihad or holy war in Gobir against what he regarded as the corrupt forms of the faith being practised there. Between 1804 and 1810 he conquered all fourteen states, established his capital at Sokoto, took the title Sarkin Musulim (Commander of the Faithful), and appointed other Fulani as emirs in each Hausa state capital.

Dan Fodio then turned his attention to the more formidable enemy of Bornu. In the mid century the king of Bornu, Ali Omarmi, had successfully fought off a Tuareg attack. His son Ahmed now had to face the Fulani, fresh from their conquest of the Hausa Bokwoi and Banza Bokwoi. He was soon dethroned, and dan Fodio destroyed the old capital of Njimi, a cherished shrine.

The Fulani only remained in control of Bornu for ten months. A religious leader gathered enough strength to expel the rather weak governor dan Fodio left behind. But this was the end of the thousand-year-long Sefuwa line of Bornu rulers; for the leader founded his own line and expelled the Sefuwa. It was this new line of rulers that the European explorers Oudney, Clapperton and Denham found on the throne when they arrived in Bornu in 1823.

Our knowledge of the Hausa and Bornu states is still very incomplete. An Italian whose real name was Giovanni Leone but who is usually known as Leo Africanus made a journey to the area to the west of Lake Chad in about 1510. He then wrote an account of his travels which he called *The History and Description of Africa and the notable Things therein contained*. Although he made some surprising mistakes in this work (for example stating that he saw the Niger flowing *westwards*), his account is still today one of our best sources of information about the area in that period.

Map 6: The Bornu and Hausa States

7

The Asante[1]

Y ou will remember how the Empire of Ghana was overthrown by the Almoravid leader Abu Bekr in 1076. It is probable that this defeat resulted in a mass flight of people of that Empire south and *south-eastwards* to escape the cruelty of their conquerors. If this is so, then almost certainly there were amongst these fleeing people the ancestors of the Akan of modern Ghana - Fante, Akim, Akwapim, Akwamu, and, most numerous of all, Asante. The Akan entered the forest zone as a single band, and then dropped away under various leaders at convenient spots along the way, in much the same way as happened with the Dagomba. The first settlement, indeed, was made just outside the forest zone, at modern Techiman.

But there is another possible origin of the Akan people. They may have come from Kanem (Bornu) near Lake Chad, and moved *south-westwards* to their present home. If so, they reached the present northern Ghana in about the eleventh century, established the Bono state about 1295, and reached the coast at about the same time. We know that the second Bonohene (King of Bono) Akumfi Ameyaw I, sent a royal prince named Obunumankoma to Mali at the head of a trade delegation, and may have visited North Africa. When Obunumankoma became Bonohene in 1363, he established gold-dust currency and gold weights of the type so popular as collectors' pieces in Asante today. He had a very long reign, and when he died in 1431 Bono-Mansu, his capital, was a large and wealthy town with a separate foreign traders' quarter where the North African caravans parked.

---

[1] A common spelling of this name has been Ashanti

Wherever they came from, the Asante vividly remember the foundation of their capital, Kumasi (originally called Okumanyinase). In much the same way, the Mende remember the foundation of many of their towns in Sierra Leone. A Dagomba hunter from Yendi is said to have set up a popular elephant meat stall under an Okumanyinase tree at this spot. As a result he gathered round him a little settlement of other hunters, and of buyers and sellers of all kinds of commodities and services; particularly as his stall was, like Yendi, on a trade artery between north and south. It was much later, however, that the first big group of Akans actually settled at Okumanyinase - not until about 1600, some 400 years after they had reached the coast. Led by a smith called Otumfi Bi, they gathered in the near-by village of Asafo, now a part of Kumasi. They had travelled via Akrokerri; but we do not know precisely why they had made the move. At this stage there were two distinct villages - Okumanyinase itself, inhabited by the Dagombas and their hangers-on, and Asafo, the village of the Akans.

Otumfi Bi was anxious to form a union, it is recalled, between the two. There was, however, a big difficulty. Whilst Dagombas passed on their property down the male line, the Akans did so down the female line. Asafo must already have had almost as many people as Okumanyinase in Otumfi Bi's day; for he felt confident enough to suggest that the Dagombas should give up *their* system of inheritance for his.

It was his successor Kwabia Amenfi, however, who is remembered as first joint chief of Asafo and Okumanyinase, and of the well-forested countryside round about. Amenfi ought therefore perhaps to be honoured as the first true ruler of the Asante capital. At this time, however, whatever their relative numbers might have been, we must remember that it was the Dagombas who were the natives (in the sense of being the first arrivals), and the Akans who were the strangers.

Amenfi's successor, Oti Akenten, who ruled in the mid-seventeenth century, is described as a member of the famous Ayoko clan of the Akan people. He had come from Asantemanso, and had bought the 'stool' (throne) from Amenfi or his heirs; for the well-known Golden Stool had not yet 'descended from heaven'. But we believe that even at this early stage the Kumasihene (King of Kumasi), as Akenten now called himself for the first time, was being ceremonially 'enstooled', much as is any modern Akan chief.

At the end of the seventeenth century the powerful Akan kingdom of Denkyera, established fifty miles south-west of Kumasi in the first half of that century, was defeated in a war with the latter town. It was this defeat that was to lead directly to the foundation of the Asante Confederacy.

Obiri Yeboa succeeded Oti Akenten as Kumasihene in 1670. He was an aggressive ruler, warring against Adanse (in about 1680), and 'persuading', by methods that were not always gentle, Ahwin and Kaase to join hands with him.

He tried this once too often, however, when he sought to bring the Domaa people of the town of Asuntiriso under his control. In the resulting war, Obiri Yeboa was defeated and killed, and when his uncle declined to succeed him, the great Osei Tutu became Kumasihene, in about 1700.

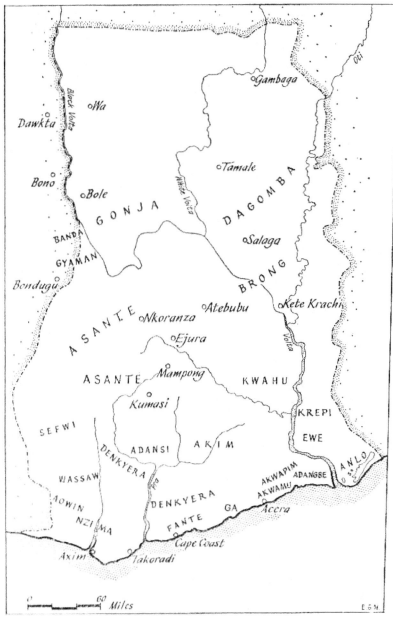

Map 7 Peoples of Ghana

All the while the area under the control of Kumasi had been growing. At the turn of the century the Amakumhene, Akosa Yiadom, was defeated and killed, and his territory was added to Kumasi's domain. Osei Tutu was one of the most interesting figures in Akan history. He was descended from a marriage between the Dagomba King Dariguenda who we believe defeated Bono in the fifteenth century, and a Bono princess. His more recent ancestors had left Bono when it was conquered by Muslim Diulas in about 1600, and had settled first in Asiakwa, and later in Asantemanso. It was from this same able clan, later called Ayokos, that Oti Akenten, first Kumasihene, had sprung.

Osei Tutu had lived in Denkyera and Akwamu, and in both towns had met a learned man named Anokye, whom he appointed his 'Prime Minister' (as we should call him today) as soon as he was enstooled. Anokye helped his royal master plan and win a war against Denkyera in the second year of his reign. This war had actually been provoked by Denkyera, whose king, Ntim Gyakari, had demanded from Kumasi a large amount of gold dust and all the town's royal wives and children; in reply for which unreasonableness he was routed at the battle of Feyase, 1701.

Anokye then decided to create a confederacy of Asante states, in order to extend very greatly the process begun by Obiri Yeboa of enlarging Kumasi's influence over the surrounding territory. So in a single year the town that had begun as an elephant meat stall under a convenient tree on a busy route gained control not only of the extensive Denkyera kingdom, but also, in effect, of the other seven Akan states near Kumasi which agreed to join the Confederacy - Mampong, Kumawu, Nsuta, Juaben, Asumegya Bekwai, and Kokofu.

It was at this fitting moment that the spirit of the Asante people caused the Golden Stool to descend from heaven, and take up residence in it, as the wise Anokye had predicted. Osei Tutu, Kumasihene, was duly elected first Asantehene, and enstooled with great pomp.

This was only the beginning of the expansion of Asante. The Domaa, the people who had defeated and killed Obiri Yeboa, were now brought to heel. The Domaa states of Abaperedase, Suman, and Gyaman all fell under Asante rule during the next thirty years. Osei Tutu had throughout these campaigns the faithful Anokye to advise him, and his advice always proved wise.

Opoku Ware, Osei Tutu's successor, continued the process of expanding the Asante kingdom. The extensive Bono Kingdom, with its capital at Bono-Masu 100 miles north of Kumasi had been, as I have mentioned,[1] one of the earliest of the Akan states to be established. After the defeat and death of the Amakuhene in about 1700, the latter's successor, Adu Denyina, fleeing from the Kumasi victors,

---

[1] P. 59

P. 3 Golden Death Mask of an Asante King, early 19th century.

was sheltered by the Bonohene, who gave him the plot of land on which Nkoranza stands today. Adu Denyina must have congratulated himself on succeeding in this way in maintaining his independence from the all-conquering Asante. His sister, left behind, was taken in marriage by Osei Tutu, however.

When a son of this marriage, Baafo Pim, visited his uncle in his new village, Adu showed his nephew with great pride a young sapling which the Bonohene himself had commanded should be planted in the centre of the settlement. The tree was an offspring of the sacred tree that stood before the Bonohene's palace in Bono-Mansu.

Unfortunately this young nephew was destined to bring disaster to the Bonohene, his uncle's protector, and to Nkoranza, his uncle's settlement. In the 1740s Baafo Pim became Nkoranzahene. His cousin Opoku Ware was Asantehene, and Ameyaw Kwaakye was Bonohene. Following a minor misunderstanding, the Bonohene's son insulted Baafo Pim in front of the latter's followers. Baafo, smarting and unforgiving, in spite of the Bonohene's personal apologies, determined to make mischief between the two powerful rulers at Bono-Mansu and Kumasi with a view to destroying the former. He succeeded only too well. Fooled by Baafo into believing that an advancing Asante crowd was coming on a peaceful mission, the people of Bono-Mansu were caught completely unprepared. There was a terrible massacre at Nkoranza, Baafo's own capital. The soldiers in Techiman, just outside Bono Mansu, withstood the Asante onslaught for a gallant week, during which the people of Bono-Mansu burnt their own capital and, led by the Bonohene's son who had started all the trouble, fled. The Bonohene committed suicide near Techiman, whilst his heir was taken by the triumphant Asante (who mistook him for the Bonohene) to Kumasi. Here he died fourteen years later. The real Bonohene's grave may still be visited outside Techiman today.

The traitor Baafo Pim survived all this. In fact he remained Nkoranzahene, as a subject chief of the Asantehene. All Bono's vast lands, stretching north as far as Krachi, were now subject to the Asante. And to these before long were added Gonja, to the north, Dagomba (in the second half of the eighteenth century, as we shall see), Akim across the Pra, and Sefwi across the Ofin.

Opoku Ware had outmatched even Osei Tutu as a builder of Asante power. Anokye, now a very old man, must also have been a very contented one. But for European gunpowder, this might have been the start of another Empire of Ghana, or Mali or Songhai . . . and the campaign against the Akim had brought the Asante within earshot of that gunpowder. For the Akim were allies of the Fanti; and both Akim and Fanti, like Edo[1] and Yoruba,[2] had fallen victim to the terribly strong temptation to deal with the European slave trader.

---

[1] P. 73
[2] P. 67

8

Oyo and Benin

(see map page 73)

T he Yoruba of Nigeria are believed by many modern historians to be descended from a people who were living on the banks of the Nile 2,000 years ago, and who were at that time in close contact with both the Egyptians and the Jews. Some time before the year A.D. 600, if this belief is correct, this people must have left their fertile lands, for reasons which we cannot now discover, and have joined in the ceaseless movement of tribes westwards and southwards across our continent. We can only guess at the many adventures they and their descendants must have had on their long journey, and at the number of generations which passed before they arrived. All we can be certain about is that they were a negro people (of which ancient Egypt probably had at least one community, as we have seen),[1] and that one of the many princely states they founded on their arrival in West Africa between the seventh and tenth centuries was Ife.

In this town there gradually developed a civilization that was to spread its influence to many other near-by states during the centuries before the Europeans arrived, particularly to Oyo and Benin. This civilization owed its strength to the fact that it blended successfully the way of life of the newcomers from the north-east with that of the natives of the area. What the newcomers brought, as we can see was the case with the Timne of Sierra Leone, was a military tradition which they had been forced to develop during their wanderings. They soon made themselves masters of Ife, and their second king, Oranyan, lies buried

P. 4 Yoruba Bronze Figure, probably of a Goddess, 17th or 18th century (from the Ogoni House, Apomu, now Nigerian Museum, Lagos).

---

[1] P. 20

P. 5 Ife Terracotta head, probably of a Queen, 13th or 14th century, Ife Museum

there today. Then some of them moved fifty miles north-west to make a fresh conquest at Oyo. Like the Asante[1] and the Mende, the Yoruba states were really small and quite separate states at first. They only joined together when forced to

---

[1] P. 59

P. 6 Typical Yoruba Wood Carving, showing four Soldiers (early 19th century)

do so for defence, or persuaded to do so for concerted attack. The Alafin (ruler) of Oyo was accepted by the people of Ife as their *political* ruler, so stern that honour required any defeated general to commit suicide rather than return to Oyo. Many of these generals in fact set up new Yoruba communities elsewhere; and so the civilization spread. The Oni (ruler) of Ife was, in return, accepted by the people of Oyo as *spiritual* ruler of both towns, and Ife remained the cultural centre of Yorubaland. Twenty years ago the famous Ife bronze masks, beautiful examples of that culture and six or seven centuries old, were discovered buried in the ground.

Oyo reached its peak in the fifteenth century. At this time it is believed to have stretched from the borders of modern Dahomey to the Niger. Then at the beginning of the seventeenth century the younger son of the ruler of Great Arda established the state of Dahomey, with its capital at Abomey. Dahomey soon subdued the coast around Ouidah, forcing chiefs there to fly north-eastwards to seek allies in Yoruba land. The Alafin of Oyo was only too pleased to oblige; for Dahomey had become a conquest worth making. He attacked and defeated King Tegbesu of Abomey in 1747, and received tribute from him, until Oyo itself collapsed.

This collapse came about because the Alafin had by now acquired more wealth and power than he knew how to use wisely. He used them, for example, to help supply the Europeans with slaves. When Yoruba chiefs and Europeans paid him well for the slaves he sold, he grew richer still. With increased wealth came increased abuse of power. In the nineteenth century Ilorin, between Oyo and the Niger, sought Fulani help in revolting against the Alafin. Just as the latter had helped the coastal chiefs of Ouidah against Abomey, so now the Fulani Akimi needed no second invitation to launch himself against Oyo. First he made sure of success by occupying Ilorin, the town that had asked for his help, and using it as a base. Then he turned against Oyo itself. Had the Alafin's rule been kindlier and wiser towards the end, he might now have found plenty of allies amongst the other Yoruba states against the feared Fulani. But the hatred and fear created

P. 7 Ife Bronze Head, probably of an Oni, 13th or 14th century, Ife Museum

amongst the Yorubas themselves by their own slave trading ran even deeper than their hatred of the Fulani. The Alafin was defeated; Oyo's power crumbled; and when the Fulani finally retreated they left behind a Yorubaland which was fast breaking up, its towns fighting each other more bitterly than ever.

The other area of modern Nigeria which fell in the middle ages under the powerful cultural influence of Ife was Benin. Yet the people of the Benin state are not Yoruba, but Edo. Unlike the Yoruba, who you will remember had a secular ruler in Oyo and a spiritual ruler in Ife, the Edo of Benin built a state which was a single, closely knit theocracy (that is, was governed by God through human agents). Edo folk-lore says that even the creation of their state was the work of God, whom they call Osanobua, as the Yoruba call him Shango, the Akan Nyame, and the Mende Ngewo. Osanobua, say the people of Benin, sent his sons to live on earth. You will notice the similarity here with Christian teaching. But that similarity does not last long. Each of Osanobua's sons was to choose something useful to take down to earth, and most of them did in fact choose physical objects or personal qualities which would obviously stand them in good stead. The youngest, however, was advised by a bird to take to earth an apparently useless snail's shell. Showing great faith, he obeyed; and so they all descended to earth. To their dismay they found it flooded - and here again we are struck by the resemblance to

P. 8 Bronze Figure of a Hunter carrying an Antelope, with his Dog. Found at Benin (origin and period unknown).

Christian teaching. None of the things brought down from the sky -'iso' - to the earth - 'agbo' - seemed now of any use, least of all the shell. The bird counsellor was still at hand, however, and told the youngest son to turn his shell upside down. As he did this an endless stream of sand fell from it and covered the waters. Thus it was that this youngest son, who became the first Oba of Benin, became also the landlord of the whole 'agbo', from whom his elder brothers had to buy or rent land on which to found other states (including the Yoruba states, say the Edo). This is obviously only folk-lore. But it resulted in the historical fact that this first ruling family became known as 'Ogie iso', 'rulers of the sky'

. After some time, however, this proud and wealthy state is described by Edo historians as running into serious difficulties from rebels within its borders. These succeeded in deposing the twelfth 'Ogie iso'. There was now a break in the succession of kings, during which Benin was a republic. The line was however resumed when the Edo chiefs sent a messenger to the Oni of Ife inviting him to send one of his sons to found a new dynasty in Benin. This, as far as we can tell, was in the thirteenth century, just before Ife reached the peak of its power, and when its rulers were looking for fresh conquests. The Oni sent a son called Araminya to Benin. Unfortunately Araminya found it very difficult to get used to the differences between the Yoruba and Edo ways of life. He decided to return home, but reported to his royal father on doing so that he had left an unborn child behind in Benin. The child's mother was probably descended from a younger brother of the last 'Ogie iso'. When the child, as everyone had hoped, was born a boy, he was joyfully crowned Oba, and given the title Eweka I. So there was established in Benin an Ife-founded ruling house which still exists today, and has supplied it with thirty-five Obas. Each Oba had three groups of councillors: a hereditary group descended from the 'Ogie iso'; 'town chiefs'; and 'palace chiefs'. Members of the latter two groups were appointed individually by the Oba; but all councillors had to combine the duties of royal adviser, civil servant, and provincial governor.

Eweka I's 'eguae' (palace) was built in a quarter of Benin called Uzama, between the two west walls; and it is here that his descendants are still crowned.

This quarter has also given its name to the seven paramount chiefs at the Oba's court, who are still known collectively as the Usama. Eweka's successor also lived in this 'eguae'. The next, Ewedo, defeated a challenger, Ogiave, in a battle which is still staged in mock form as soon as the eldest son (or, in the absence of sons, brother) of a dead Oba has ceremonially buried his predecessor and proclaimed himself the new ruler of Benin. Even the ceremonial division of the land between the representatives of Ewedo and Ogiave is still observed today, after the mock battle.

Ewedo's share of the land included the site of the present Oba's palace, on which Ewedo built a now demolished palace. His successor, Oguola, no doubt conscious of the fate of the last 'Ogie iso', and noticing with alarm the rapid growth of the power of Udo, a town thirty miles away, built a defensive wall around his capital.

But it seems that enemies such as Udo were not able to prevent the people of Benin and Ife from meeting and sharing their way of life. We believe that it was during the reign of Oguola that the well-known 'lost wax' or 'cire perdue' method of bronze casting was introduced to Benin City from Ife. Like all craftsmen in Benin (and the city had workers in wood, leather, iron, ivory, and

P. 9 Typical Bronze Plaque of two Musicians striking gongs, Benin, 16th or 17the century, from the old King's Palace, Benin (now in Nigerian museum, Lagos)

cloth), the brass-smiths were organized into a highly disciplined guild, living in its own street. The blacksmiths' street was called Igueroyo. They did not dare make or sell a cast without the permission of the Oba himself. So it is likely that the Oba had received the secret of making these castings direct from the Oni, and so was in a position to keep a particularly strict control over the practice of this precious craft. Many of the objects cast were ceremonial, and a new Oba would always make the first casting on a specially reserved site. The method used was to make a wax moulding, of the exact shape and size desired for the final cast, round a clay kernel. The wax moulding was then coated with another thick layer of clay, so that the wax was sandwiched between the two layers of clay. The whole apparently shapeless mass was then heated until the wax had melted and could be drained out (i.e. 'lost') from a small hole pierced in the outer layer of clay. Finally molten bronze was poured through this hole until it filled the cavity thus left, and the clay was broken away when the bronze had set.

As Benin reached the height of its power in the fifteenth and sixteenth centuries, it gradually shook off its dependence on Ife. But this was a slow process; for in 1485 the Portuguese found that although Benin was then a very powerful state the new

P. 10 Bronze Figure of a Chief, probably 18th century, from Udo, near Benin (now in Nigerian Museum, Lagos)

Oba still had to be recognized, at least formally, by Oghene as the Edo call the

Oni. But unfortunately Benin, like Oyo, was now being corrupted by too much power and greed. Military expansion rather than art interested Obas such as Ewuare, Ozolua, Esigie, Orhogbua, and Ehegbuda. They succeeded in extending Benin's frontiers until they reached Idah(a town on the Niger conquered by Esigie in 1520) in the north and Ouidah on the coast to the west. The Edo claim to have founded Lagos, and that Orhogbua made it his military headquarters in the middle of the sixteenth century. There is strong evidence that just as the present Benin ruling family was founded by the son of an Oni of Ife, so the present Lagos ruling family was founded in the middle of the sixteenth century by the son of Oba Orhogbua of Benin. A century later the Oba was described as having a reserve army of 100,000 at his command. But alas! the European slave trade with its 'get-rich-quick' lure was to prove as fatal to Benin as to Oyo[1] - not so much in the numbers of strong men snatched away in their prime, but in the number of rulers corrupted in their attitudes. Not only were the Obas now supplying slaves, animal skins and pepper to the coastal traders, but they also controlled much of the flow of *all* trade between Yorubaland and the coast. All this easy wealth inevitably led to civil strife and endless wars of succession. Although there were brief periods of revival under exceptionally able Obas, a gradual decline now set in, which permitted the British to capture a thoroughly corrupt and demoralized Benin City in 1897, and depose Overami, the Oba.

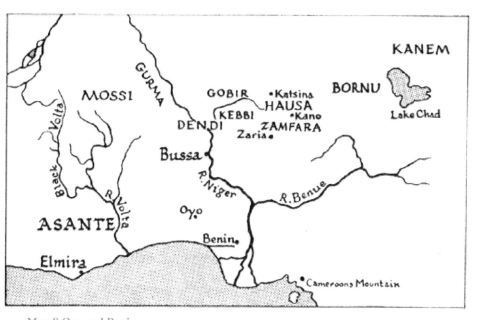

Map 8 Oyo and Benin

---

[1] P. 68

Part Two: The Arrival of the Europeans

9

The Fifteenth Century – Charts and Caravels

a. SENEGAMBIA

The Gambia, as you will see from the map on page99, has an unusual shape, consisting of little more than the banks of the river after which it is named. It is almost surrounded by Senegal, and so this area used to be known as 'Senegambia'.

The main peoples living in this area today are the Mandingo, Joloff, Fula and Jola. The Mandingo have their home in the Manding region of Senegal, 750 miles east of modern Bathurst, and are now to be found on both banks of the Gambia River. The Joloff's ancient kingdom of Sine Salum once stretched 100 miles inland from the Atlantic coast. The Joloff people are particularly handsome, their women being noted for their height and elegance; but they are not the original inhabitants of the Gambia and Senegal region where we find them today. They invaded it from the east some time during the period we covered earlier on. The Fula or Fulani are a people we met in Chapters 4[1] and 6[2], and are today to be found in considerable numbers in many West African countries. These include Guinea (where lie the Futa Jallon Mountains, the original home of many of them) and all the former British colonies. They reached the Gambia even later than the Joloff, but we do know that by 1620 they were in the area where the Senegal and Gambia rivers rise. These early Fula arrivals were peace-loving, unlike the Fula who followed them and who were fiercely aggressive. Another important division we must remember within the Fula people is the religious one. Some Fula are Muslim, and these are known as the Tukolor Fula; but the majority are pagan. Finally, there are the Jola. These are a rather primitive people, using that word in the sense in which I have defined it in the preface. But they are also the true natives of the Gambia, since, as far as we can tell at present, they have lived in the region longer than any of the other peoples I have mentioned. However, being both smaller in numbers and more peaceful in nature than the Mandingo, they were conquered by them. The Jola, like many of the Fula, are pagan. Each of these peoples was more than a group of persons who merely spoke the same language. Although their kingdoms were never as extensive or wealthy as the empires of Ghana, Mali and Songhai, some of these coastal peoples had developed their system of government well beyond the village level. The Mandingo, for example, had four small kingdoms along the north bank of the Gambia River. Moving eastwards, these were Niumi or Barra, Baddibu, Niani and Wuli. 'Niani' will remind us at once of the capital[3] of the Empire of Mali; and of course the Mandingo were once rulers of Mali and were Mande-speaking. Then on the south bank the Mandingo had seven kingdoms: Kombo, Kiang, Jarra, Niamina, Eropina, Jimara, and Tomani.

It was to such kingdoms that the Europeans came. Henry the Navigator, son of John I of Portugal and Philippa, daughter of the English John of Gaunt, founded his naval academy at Sagres in Portugal in 1419. Using two- and three-masted caravels with triangular lateen sails which enabled them to tack, his sailors explored a little more of the coast of West Africa each year. Madeira had already been discovered in 1418. In 1434 Gil Eannes rounded the fearsome Cape Bojador. Cape Blanco was passed seven years later. In 1442 the first gold, and ten slaves, were taken by Gonçalves from Rio De Oro (the river of gold) to Portugal; and at once the pace quickened. In 1443 Arguin was reached, and two years later Nuno Tristao rounded what he called delightedly Cape Verde (the green cape); for the hot glare of the desert here began to give way to the moist smile of the forest.

---

[1] P. 41
[2] P. 56
[3] P. 33

Nuno did in fact go ashore here. He made a treaty of friendship and commerce with the people of Cape Verde, and there after there were annual trade missions from Portugal to this region. Then in 1447 Nuno pushed farther south, passing the mouth of the Gambia in 1448, but failing to notice it because he was a long way from the coast. Reaching the Rio Grande, 100 miles to the south, he was killed by hostile people with whom he tried to negotiate a treaty similar to the one he had made at Cape Verde.

Henry the Navigator was not discouraged by this loss. He had begun sponsoring exploration of the Guinea coast (as it was soon to be known) as a result of hearing stories, whilst fighting the Moors in North Africa, of the great abundance of Guinea gold. Now more stories reached him, this time from the people of Cape Verde. They told how gold mined on the banks of the Gambia was sent overland to Spain. Henry determined to redouble his efforts to reach and divert to Portugal this flow of wealth. It is probable that he also wished to make converts for the Catholic Church and widen the frontiers of geographical knowledge, but there is little doubt that with him the economic motive was the most powerful one.

So in 1455 Henry sent two expeditions to the Gambia. One was under the command of the Venetian Luiz de Cadamosto, and consisted of one ninety-ton ship. The other consisted of two ships under the command of the Genoese Antoniotto Usodimare in 1456. Joining hands near Cape Verde, Cadamosto and Usodimare became the first Europeans whom we know to have seen the Gambia River. It was a brief glimpse: set upon by suspicious inhabitants of estuary villages (probably Mandingo), the Portuguese commanders were persuaded by their crews to go home for reinforcements before attempting the search for gold which was the object of their voyage.

The following year Cadamosto and Usodimare returned with a stronger force, still under the patronage of Prince Henry. They sailed twenty miles up the Gambia River, and reached an island which they could see at once effectively controlled the passage upstream. When one of their sailors had to be buried on this island they named it St Andrews after him; today it is called James Island. Leaving behind a simple cross to mark their comrade's grave and no doubt mystify passing fishermen, the Portuguese sailed farther upstream, reaching what is today the Baddibu district on the north bank. Here for eleven days they parleyed with Chief Battimansa (you will recall that 'mansa' means Emperor),[1] and exchanged presents and information. The exchanging of presents was in fact plain bartering, cheap articles of European origin being exchanged for slaves and a little gold - much less gold than the visitors had hoped to find. But they did meet another king, Numimansa, King of Niumi (Barra) on the northern bank of the mouth of the Gambia, who had perhaps seen the caravels pass and followed

[1] P. 36

them inquisitively upstream. Satisfied that they had at least established useful contacts as well as made a little profit, the Europeans returned home, calling at the River Casamance on the way.

In 1458 Prince Henry sent out a third expedition to the Gambia; and this seems to prove that, however disappointing the amount of gold brought back by the previous expedition, its financial profit had been at least encouraging. The new commander was Diego[1] Gomes, a man who seems to have seen nothing inconsistent about accepting presents of slaves whilst preaching the love of God. He set a pattern to be followed, as we shall see, by many others, including John Newton. Gomes anchored off St Andrews, the little burial island we noted earlier. Then, sailing on upstream past Sikka Point, he was able to secure the first really substantial amount of gold the Portuguese had obtained in West Africa - 180 lb. of dust given to him by a north-bank chief named Frangazick in exchange for European goods. With a guide he moved farther upstream still, to Niumi, Wuli and Kantora, leaving one of his caravels at each place (see map on page 99). At Kantora a trader from North Africa was found who told Gomes of rich gold mines farther on in the interior. But, tantalizing as this sounded, Gomes could not go any farther on this trip. His ships were strung out dangerously along the river between St. Andrews and Kantora, his men were exhausted by the unaccustomed heat and by the increasing difficulty of navigating in a narrowing channel. So Gomes headed downstream once more. He obtained from Battimansa on the way a promise of safe conduct for all Europeans, and also some slaves, in exchange for wine and biscuits. He sent a messenger into Joloff country, and the man returned with ivory and slaves - a present, he said, from a Joloff king. His appetite for wealth blunted, the Portuguese commander now gave a display of religious zeal. He described the Catholic Church so enthusiastically that Numimansa was persuaded to get rid of his Muslim advisers and declare himself ready for Christian baptism. Gomes undertook to ask his master to send a priest next time.

Gomes must have kept his word, for Henry did send out an abbot, who seems to have arrived after the death of this particular Numimansa. The Abbot occupied himself with building the earliest church of which we have a record in West Africa: the church of San Domingo at Juffure, on the north bank opposite James Island. Converts were few; but at least the dead sailor's cross on the island had found a living, lofty reflection across the water.

But Henry's own end was near. He died in November 1460. He had left three important structures behind. The church of San Domingo, reminding the world that his motives were not entirely mercenary, was one. Another was the beginnings of a castle on Arguin Island, a reminder that the strength of the soldier lay behind the greed of the trader and the zeal of the churchman. The third

---

[1] Portuguese form Diogo

was the academy at Sagres, a guarantee that the scientific knowledge which had been won would be preserved and applied.

So Henry's work was now continued largely by the King of Portugal himself, Afonso V. Particularly anxious not to give his Spanish neighbours any advantage in the Guinea trade (you will remember the reports Prince Henry's men had heard from the people of Cape Verde of Spanish overland trade in gold with Guinea),[1] Afonso gave a contract to a rich Lisbon trader named Fernao Gomes to explore at least 100 leagues[2] of the Guinea coast annually in return for a monopoly of its trade.

On his first expedition Gomes stopped at Cape Verde, and here learnt that the Spanish were buying slaves, gold, ivory, pepper and hides from the Joloff, and were selling them arms with which to defend themselves against the Portuguese! Gomes determined to put a stop to this. He waylaid a Spanish ship engaged in this traffic near Cape Verde, took its captain, de Prado, back to Portugal, and had him burnt as a heretic.

The Portuguese were now able to expand their trade with the Cape Verde and Gambia people. In 1466 the people of the Cape Verde Islands were given the same monopoly over trade as far as Sierra Leone, as Fernão Gomes was to be given beyond Sierra Leone in 1469. These Cape Verde Islanders were largely Portuguese settlers, and are not to be confused with the Joloff of the mainland near Cape Verde. It was these settlers who were later to be the first to use this monopoly as a source of slaves for the transatlantic market - an even more wicked traffic than that which took slaves to Portugal. For whereas the slaves taken north were relatively well treated in the homes in which they served as domestics, those who were to go westwards later died in large numbers on board their ships or under the gruelling working conditions of the American and Caribbean plantations. Yet others, only a little less unfortunate, were later taken south by the Cape Verde Islanders to São Tome, where they were used as labour on sugar plantations whose products went to Portugal, and from there to other countries of Europe.

Up to this point, 1466, it seems that relations between the Europeans and the peoples of the Gambia were fairly good, and certainly much better than the relations between Portuguese and Spanish on the coast. But in 1475 the Spanish made the bad mistake, from the point of view of their own interests, of taking slaves by force instead of buying or bartering for them, and of abducting a Mandingo king as well. When the Spanish king, Ferdinand V, was presented with these 'prizes' by the captains of the three caravels which had taken them, he was quick to release the king. But he sold the 100 other captives into slavery in Spain; and from then on the Europeans met opposition in one form or another from the

---

[1] P. 77

[2] A league is approximately three miles.

kings of the Gambia when they came in search of slaves. Matters were, however, made easier for Portugal by an agreement signed in 1480 between Portugal and Spain. Under this agreement Portugal's monopoly of the Guinea trade was recognized by Spain, in return for the cession by Portugal to Spain of the Canary Islands. Portugal now guarded this monopoly very jealously. When she heard in 1482 that Edward IV of England was to allow an English expedition to sail to Guinea, Portugal protested very vigorously, and the English had to abandon the idea. Also in 1482 John II of Portugal completed the castle on Arguin Island which had been begun by his predecessor Afonso V in Henry the Navigator's day. It was ready just in time: the following year a new European challenger to the Portuguese monopoly on the Guinea coast appeared — the French. In that year they reached Cape Verde for the first time, and moved steadily down the coast in later years, as we shall see.

But the Portuguese had had a very long start. By 1484 one of their sailors, Diego Cam,[1] had reached the Congo. On the way he called at the Gambia, and has recorded an observation that although gold was obtainable more easily farther down the coast, pepper, or 'malaguetta', was plentiful and cheap on the Gambia.

We have seen the first major mistake made by the Europeans in Guinea - that of taking away slaves against the will of the kings. Towards the end of this century they made their second mistake - that of interfering in local politics in Senegal and the Gambia. What they did was to offer to support one claimant for a throne against his brother on condition that their candidate become a Christian. This candidate, who was a Joloff called Bemoi, at first declined the offer, but later accepted it because it seemed the only way to obtain the military strength he needed to secure the throne. In 1487 he was taken to Lisbon, was baptized and presented to King John II of Portugal. Now the Portuguese had to keep their side of the bargain. They sent twenty warships under Pedro Vaz da Cunha to Senegal with Bemoi (now renamed John), who was made king. But, as was only to be expected, this uncomfortable alliance soon broke up. The Portuguese insisted on building a fort at the mouth of the river against Bemoi's wishes. When he objected da Cunha arranged to have him murdered. But the Portuguese were eventually the losers, as the Joloff never trusted them again.

We must note one more Portuguese expedition to the Gambia-Senegal area during the fifteenth century. In 1491 Rodrigo Rebello led an expedition of seven to the Mandingo ruler of Kantora, which you will remember as the farthest point reached up the River Gambia by the earlier expeditions (page 77). Here he was received by the Mandimansa, or Mandingo ruler of Kantora, and there was the usual exchange of cheap European products for valuable Guinea gold and ivory. There is no mention of slaves being taken away from the Gambia for the next

---

[1] The Portuguese form is Diogo Cäo.

few years, at any rate, even though the Treaty of Tordesillas (1494) gave papal approval to the Portuguese monopoly.

b. SIERRA LEONE

In Sierra Leone, as in the Gambia, the Europeans found many peoples, at varying stages of political development, and none with the well-advanced machinery of government, or with the large areas of territory and numbers of subject people, of the empires we have already studied. Along the coast to the north and south of the broad estuary of the Sierra Leone River were the Bullom or Sherbro. They have given their name to the Bullom shore in the north, and to Sherbro Island in the south. Along the banks of the River Scarcies were the Temne people, their largest town, according to the earliest literate visitors, being Kasseh. The Bullom and the Temne had, until the arrival of the Mende in relatively recent times, the largest states in the region. But whereas the Susu, with their cousins the Yalunka, and the Mende all belong to the Mande-speaking group of West African peoples (which also includes the Vai and Mandingo), the Bullom belong to what is called the West Atlantic group. These are linguistic or language groups, however; and although it is often useful for the student of history to be able to remember to which linguistic group a particular people belongs, we need not concern ourselves here with the significance of the groupings.

The Susu you will remember as having defeated the Empire of Ghana in 1203 and then having themselves been <u>overthrown by Mali in 1240</u>.[1] It must have been some time during the next century or two that sections of their now scattered people reached what is now Sierra Leone. They settled, early visitors record, twelve or more leagues from the coast, behind the Bullom. Of the remaining peoples we know the Limba to have been amongst the earliest arrivals, certainly earlier than the Susu and perhaps as early as the Bullom and Temne. Finally there is the group of much later arrivals, dominated by the powerful and virile Mende, and including the Kono, Vai, Koranko, Kissi and Krim.

But fifteenth-century Sierra Leone belonged to the Temne, Loko, Limba, Yalunka, Bullom and Susu. These were at the time all subject to the authority of an empire called by the Portuguese that of the Capeo or Sapi people (page 106), about which we know very little. At any rate, it seems to have survived throughout this century and part of the next, but to have disappeared before the Mende invasions.

---

[1] Chap. 3

So it was that as Prince Henry's sailors made their way ever farther down the Guinea coast in the middle of this century, the people with whom they first made contact in the area we now know as Sierra Leone were the Bullom. Alvaro Fernandes first sighted their coast in 1446. In 1462 Pedro da Sintra mapped that coast, and his voyage was later described by the same Cadamosto who had explored the Gambia River with Usodimare in 1456 (page 76). Since Cadamosto was a Venetian, he tended to use the Italian names, not the Portuguese; and today we are left with some oddly scrambled names, such as 'Sierra Leone' itself, which is a mixture of Spanish and misspelt Italian. We do not really know why the hills of this picturesque peninsula were likened to lions, but it may be that some early voyager compared their outline as seen from the harbour to that of a crouching lion, or the name may have come from the roar of thunder in the hill-tops.

The English soon followed in the wake of the Portuguese. In 1481 John Tintan and William Fabian called briefly at the anchorage at the foot of the 'Lion Mountains', in what was later realised to be the finest natural harbour in West Africa. But it was left to the Portuguese to build the first fort here, as they had done at Arguin. Between 1482 and 1495 they worked away steadily at this construction, on Tombo Island, nine miles upstream from Tagrin Point on the Sierra Leone River. It was pulled down soon after completion, presumably because the volume of trade in the area did not justify the cost of maintaining it. We shall see how a third fort built by the Portuguese at about the same time, that of São Jorge da Mina (page 82) on what was later to become the Gold Coast, does seem to have proved worth maintaining, and, unlike the others, has survived in almost continuous use until today.

At Port Loko, in the north-west of modern Sierra Leone, the Portuguese founded their main trading base, and found the local Temne very ready to do business with them. These Temne had their main settlements at Rotumba and Robaga, and the goods exchanged were very similar to those in the Gambia - gold, slaves, ivory, pepper and hides, for trinkets, cloth, alcohol and, in the following centuries, guns.

C. THE GOLD COAST

The Portuguese had reached Sierra Leone just about the time of Prince Henry's death (1460). They then moved restlessly onwards, passing the following year along what was to become later the coast of Liberia. In 1469 Fernão Gomes secured his monopoly of trade beyond Sierra Leone (page 78), and progress was even more rapid. In 1471 two of his captains, Joao de Santarem and Pedro de Esobar, passed Cape Three Points and landed somewhere between that cape and the modern Cape Coast. They soon discovered a river which, whilst not nearly as wide at its mouth as the Gambia or Sierra Leone, promised access to the interior and to its supposed wealth. Naming the river Rio São Joao (it was later renamed the Pra), they set up their trading factory at Shama near its mouth.

This time the Portuguese had really struck wealth. There was much more gold here than in either of the two other regions of Sierra Leone and Senegambia. Gomes was soon able to retire a wealthy man. He sold his monopoly back to the Portuguese king, John II, who had succeeded Afonso in 1481. It was now that the fortress of São Jorge da Mina was begun near the town of Dondou. No expense or pains were spared to make this fortification really stout enough to protect the foothold established in such promising country. Shaped stones were brought all the way from Portugal to the building site twenty miles east of Shama, and we can call Elmina Castle, as it is known today, West Africa's first partly prefabricated building. Names famous today were to be found amongst the crews of the ships comprising the convoy carrying building materials to Elmina - Bartholomew Dias and Christopher Columbus; and there is little doubt that this was an exciting project for the Europeans.

Once built, Elmina Castle became the centre of a very profitable trade. Gold and slaves were exchanged in steadily increasing volume for cloth, old linen, beads, shells, utensils and ornaments. One-twentieth of this gold was given to the Porrtuguese crown. Slaves from Benin, São Tomé[1] and Arguin were often taken there to be sold to slavers, and there was enough business in the area to justify keeping about sixty Portuguese in the fort.

It did, however, arouse some hostility amongst the Africans affected. The local king, Caramansa (the Portuguese seem to have added the suffix 'mansa' indiscriminately to the names of kings all along this coast), had been quite happy to trade, but naturally did not welcome a foreign-owned fortification on his land. Before passing on we may note the tribes that the Portuguese met on the Gold Coast. On the central coast of modern Ghana there were the Fante, who belong to the same group (the Akan) as the inland Asante. Farther east there are the Ga of what are now the Accra plains. In the extreme east are to be found the Ewe people, and in the extreme west of the coastal area the Nzima. Between these two extremes were many other peoples. The most important at this time were the Axim west of Cape Three Points, and east of that cape were the Ahanta, Comani, Efutu and Agona. (Map of Ghana page 61)

The Portuguese commander, Don Diego de Azambuja, had ten caravels, two transports, a small pinnace, 500 soldiers and seamen and 100 engineers and workmen - eloquent proof the importance his royal master attached to the 'strike' of gold. Faced with such impressive strength, Caramansa gave in to the demands of Azambuja for permission to build. Some of the Elmina people were not quite

---

[1] This is sometimes given as São Thomé or S. Thomé.

so easily cowed, however, and attacked the workers - without much success. Azambuja completed the first stage of the work, made himself comfortable in the castle with sixty men and sent the rest home with a rich cargo of gold and slaves. There was great rejoicing by the invaders at their success in at last tapping the real wealth of Guinea: King John added 'Lord of Guinea' to his royal titles, and Azambuja a castle to his coat of arms. Fresh expeditions went out from Lisbon, and other forts soon began to rise elsewhere along the coast - at Shama, the original landing place of the invaders; at Axim; and at Accra.

Since greed for wealth had brought rival traders to the less profitable Gambia and Sierra Leone, the Portuguese could surely not have expected to be left unchallenged on the aptly named 'Gold' Coast for any length of time. In fact, Elmina was built just as much to ward off attack from the sea as from the land, as its layout shows. As the century drew to a close, it was the French whose sails appeared increasingly frequently on the horizon, in defiance of the Portuguese monopoly, to which, as we have seen, the Pope lent his great authority by the Treaty of Tordesillas in 1494 (page 80). Two years before that treaty was signed we learn of French privateers capturing a Portuguese trading vessel bound from Elmina to Lisbon with holds full of gold bars and dust. And this French ship was under the command of a rebel Portuguese captain!

However, there is no doubt that the Portuguese made most of the running in the early stages of the race to enrich European countries at the expense of West Africa. Even after Bartholomew Dias had sailed to South Africa in 1487 and Vasco da Gama to India ten years later, the lure of the East, for so long the goal of all European voyages of discovery, was not strong enough to divert Portugal's attention from Guinea. Some traders and explorers, it is true, called in at Arguin, Tombo and Elmina only in order to take on supplies, and then continued their journey. But there were also others who were satisfied to look no farther than Guinea for their trade. Around the turn of the century two convoys a year shuttled between Lisbon and Elmina. Anyone caught breaking the Portuguese monopoly was promptly put to death. But if a stranger did get away with his booty the rewards were so great that privateers and interlopers, as they were called, grew year by year both in numbers and in audacity.

The Portuguese had made an interesting military mistake, moreover, at Elmina, and one which was to cost them dear during the following centuries. Failing to realize that the range of cannon was certain to increase as these weapons were improved, they did not trouble to secure a hill just to the north of that on which their fortress was built, and which overlooks it. For the time being they could feel secure behind the thick walls of São Jorge da Mina and regard the near-by hill as merely picturesque. But this was to be an error on their part as bad as the abduction of slaves and meddlesome interference in politics which we noted in the Gambia (page 78). And the chain of forts along the coast of modern Ghana reminds us that the Portuguese were never as successful at establishing peaceful relations with the peoples here as they were elsewhere on the Guinea coast. The forts also remind us that the trade here, being largely in gold, was more valuable than anywhere else on the coast.

d. THE SLAVE COAST

For two years after the death of Prince Henry in 1460 the exploration of the Guinea coast continued vigorously. But between 1462 and 1470 there was a lull in exploration, and the Portuguese concentrated on expanding trade with the stretch of coast they had already discovered, that is as far as modern Liberia. After Fernão Gomes won his contract in 1469 he began to make preparations for a new period of exploration, which in fact began in 1471. Between that year and 1480, when war between Portugal and Castile interrupted exploration once more, another long stretch of coast was visited by the Portuguese sailors for the first time, from the Volta to the Niger. It is this stretch which is known as the Slave Coast.

The Portuguese king during this period of renewed activity was Afonso V, who died in 1481. First of all, Fernão do Po reached the island now named after him, but which was originally named Ilha Fermoso. This was in 1472-3. Soon after, one of Afonso's knights, Ruy de Sequeira, visited São Tomé, Cape Catherine and O Principe. The latter island was originally named St Antonio, as it was discovered on St Anthony's Day, January 17, 1474. Pedro da Cintra, who had reached Sierra Leone in 1460 (page 81), was probably one of the captains who sailed with Fernão do Po in the early 1470s. By 1475, when Gomes' contract expired, the coast from Elmina to Cape St Catherine was known to the Portuguese, and they now began to explore it thoroughly, particularly the Benin area. From 1474 onwards Prince John, the son of Afonso V, was given responsibility for the administration of all the trade of the Guinea coast. For the first year or so after he had been given this responsibility he delegated it to Gomes, but after 1475 he exercised it himself.

We get from various authors glimpses of this trade between Portugal and what is today the coast of Nigeria, and the islands just off that coast. A Flemish trader called de la Fosse was on the coast of Mina in 1479 when he saw two Portuguese caravels commanded by Fernão do Po sail past on their way to the Rio dos Esclavos (River of Slaves), 200 leagues farther on, and five leagues east of the Benin River (Rio Fermoso). The following year they returned with a cargo of slaves, who were sold at Mina. This seems to have been quite a common practice at this time. Slaves from the Benin coast and nearby islands were sold at Elmina to traders who took them either to the New World or Europe. A fort was built by the Portuguese at Gwato near the mouth of the Benin River to protect the

84

main source of these slaves. Yet other slaves were brought from the Congo to São Tome, and either joined those bound for Mina or were kept to work on the plantations on São Tome itself.

When John II succeeded Afonso V as King of Portugal in 1481 the exploration of the hinterland behind the Slave Coast began, the fort at Gwato being used as a base. The first peppers from Guinea were taken to John from this country, and he must have been pleased to find a source of this much-valued spice which was not as distant nor as difficult to tap as the East. In 1483 Fernão do Po and others visited Benin, and in 1485 so did Diego Cam, on his way back from the Congo. The King of Benin was impressed by these visitors, it seems; for he now sent an envoy from Gwato to Portugal to ask John to send him priests. When these arrived in 1486, however, they failed to convert him to Christianity.

The Gwato fort does not seem to have been quite as much of a success as had been hoped, certainly not as much so as the Elmina fort. It was closed at about this time (1486), although the slave trade between Benin and the Elmina market, often via São Tome, continued. The São Tome islanders were given permission in 1485 to trade direct with the mainland instead of doing so through the Portuguese captains. Quite a large colony had settled on São Tome Island by now, including many Jews from Portugal and other parts of Europe fleeing before religious persecution. There were also a number of convicts, exiles (voluntary and otherwise) and fugitives from justice. A certain Fernão de Mello, who was captain of the island until his death in 1522, introduced sugar to the island, and so laid the basis of its great prosperity in the next century. The soil was well suited to the sugar cane, and there was a plentiful supply of labour in the form of slaves from the near-by Benin and Congo coasts. Many of the settlers grew wealthy, built large mansions and lived very comfortable lives in a type of feudal society.

Let us finally, however, see how the people of the Benin mainland were living at the time. The Portuguese author of the work from which much of our knowledge of this coast at this time comes, the *Esmeraldo de situ orbis*, was named Duarte Pacheco Pereira. It was written in about 1507 by a man who seems to have had extensive personal knowledge of Guinea. Here is his description of Gwato, the port which served Benin: 'A league up this river [Fermoso, or Benin] on the left two tributaries enter the main stream; if you ascend the second of these for twelve leagues you find a town called Huguatoo [Gwato], of some 2,000 inhabitants; this is the harbour of the great city of Beny, which lies nine leagues in the interior along a good road. Small ships of fifty tons can go as far as Huguatoo. This city is about a league long from gate to gate; it has no wall but is surrounded by a large moat, very wide and deep, which suffices for its defence. I was there four times. Its houses are made of mud walls covered with palm leaves. The kingdom of Benin is about eighty leagues long and forty wide; it is usually at war with its neighbours and takes many captives, whom we buy at twelve or fifteen brass bracelets each, or for copper bracelets which they prize more.'

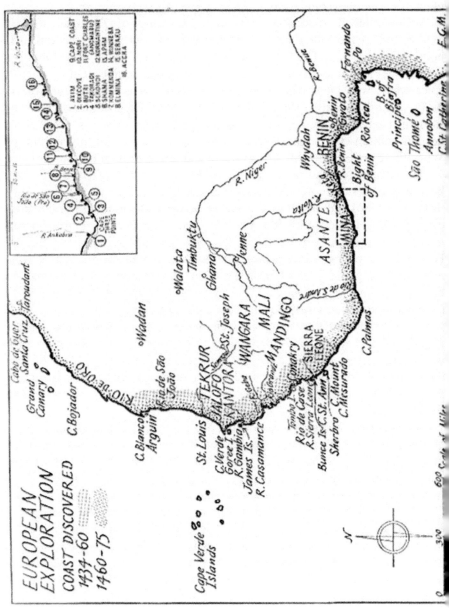

Map 9 European Exploration

This does not tell us a great deal. But we are left with an impression of a disturbed land and a city on the defensive, surrounded by enemies, visited by unscrupulous traders. We can only hope that behind the moat, within at least some of those mud walls, there were to be found some craftsmen who had both the leisure and the incentive to practice the precious art of bronze casting we learnt about in Chapter 8, and whose works of art are so much sought after by museums in Africa, Europe and America today.

And what about the countries of Europe who had sent the visitors to Guinea and either started or made worse the disastrous raiding of tribe by tribe for slaves? As the fifteenth century drew to a close, the powerful Tudors had begun to establish their autocratic but enlightened rule upon a land previously racked with the suffering and loss caused by the Wars of the Roses. The war we have noted between Spain and Portugal was one of a long series of challenges to Portugal's strength at the end of the fifteenth and throughout the sixteenth centuries, challenges which met with increasing success. French, English, Dutch and Swedes were all at one time or another during the following century to gain in wealth drawn from the Guinea trade at the expense of the founders of that trade, the Portuguese.

10

The Sixteenth Century - Rosaries and Sea-Dogs

(see maps pages 86and 99)

a. SENEGAMBIA

As we have seen (page 77), at the start of the sixteenth century the European explorers of the Gambia had reached Kantora, and had begun the doubly evil practice of *stealing* slaves from the villages along the banks. We also saw that the Portuguese had had their monopoly on this coast challenged, first by the Spanish, then by the French; and finally strengthened by receiving papal sanction in the Treaty of Tordesillas (1494) (page 80).

For the first few decades of this century the French and Spanish interlopers, now joined by the English, were unable to prevent the Portuguese from making their way steadily up the Senegal and Gambia rivers. Later the Portuguese found the Niger and Timbuktu, and so came into contact with the Mali Empire of which we learnt in Chapter 4, and which was then in its decline. On the Gambia itself the number of Portuguese visitors was increasing steadily. Following the establishment of the church of San Domingo at Juffure opposite James Island (page 77), more and more Portuguese missionaries came out to try to make converts to the Catholic Church. In addition to the missionaries and explorers, many traders arrived; some of them were interested only in obtaining slaves, whilst others were looking for gold, ivory and the other natural products of the area, instead of, or as well as, for slaves.

A few of these missionaries and traders stayed long enough on the Gambia to justify our calling them 'settlers'. There were small Portuguese communities at Povoacao de Blancos (town of white men) near Dog Island, at Cassau, and in Kantora, for example; and their members visited Setucoo to buy gold and slaves from the Mandingo there. Some of these Portuguese traders, probably those who did not steal slaves, took African wives, and borrowed the customs and learnt the languages of their wives, who in return borrowed and learnt similarly from their husbands. The Joloff women of the Gambia still show in the way they dress, and practically all the coastal peoples of West Africa show in the way they speak, the effects of this early mingling of African and European cultures. The missionaries, however, were much less successful than the traders in getting themselves accepted by the Gambian villagers: there were few converts here, and the churches were almost entirely used by the settlers themselves.

In addition to San Domingo, there was such a church at Tankular, and another at Geregia, which may be a corruption of the Portuguese word for 'church'. From the sixteenth to the eighteenth century the King of Portugal maintained twelve priests in these Gambian churches, and ceased to do so only when it was discovered that the churches were often left unattended although salaries were being claimed by the priests.

Even the Portuguese on the Gambia in this century were not all Christians, however. Some of them were Jews, who had fled or been driven from Portugal as a result of the Catholic persecution of non-Catholics which is known as the Inquisition. We may be sure they kept far away from San Domingo and the other churches.

Meanwhile Portugal's rivals for the trade of the West African coast were pressing their claims to a share of it with more and more determination. Spanish, English and French interlopers increased steadily in number and daring. The Portuguese fought back. They divided the coast of Upper Guinea into five sections or 'trades': Arguin, Senegal, Gambia and Cantor, rivers of Guinea, and Sierra Leone. Each of these 'trades' was let on contract to a trader or firm of traders, who paid the Portuguese Crown a fixed sum for the privilege of monopoly.

In addition to this tactical step, the Portuguese took diplomatic steps to defend their monopoly. At the Peace of Cambrai in 1529 they succeeded in persuading the French to agree to order their interlopers away from the Guinea coast. But we know the French had begun twelve years later to attack this monopoly, and both in 1541 and 1559 we hear of French ships making successful trading voyages to the coast, whilst in 1570 a French ship had to be driven down the Gambia River by two Portuguese vessels, and lost thirty men. The English had no intention of being left behind in the challenging of the Portuguese monopoly. In 1530, 1553 and 1557 William Hawkins made his famous voyages from Plymouth to the Guinea coast, carrying knives, hatchets and ear-rings to exchange for ivory and pepper. These latter commodities he carried in turn across the Atlantic to the new Portuguese possessions in Brazil, and exchanged them there for dye-wood. The strange thing is that he could have saved himself the second leg of his journey; for, had he only known it, he could have obtained all the dye-wood he wanted in West Africa itself, as anyone who has seen the numerous, exquisitely tidy piles of this wood in Kroo Bay, Freetown, will know.

William Hawkins was soon followed by other 'sea-dogs', as their daring impudence led them to be called. One of these was William's son, John Hawkins, who made his first voyage in 1562. Unlike his father, John was a slave trader. He took many slaves from the Gambia and other parts of West Africa to the West Indies and the Spanish mainland of Central and South America - the Spanish Main, as it was called then. At vast profit he exchanged these slaves for hides, sugar and silver, eventually becoming, as a result, one of the richest men in England. Elizabeth I of England, who had come to the throne four years before his first voyage, benefited secretly from the profits made by the sea-dogs at the expense of the Spanish and Portuguese; although publicly she sometimes forbade her subjects to trade in the areas claimed by other nations, or to attack their shipping. The English did not show much interest in the coast north of the Gambia, however, whereas the other Europeans vied with one another along the whole West African coast.

In 1578 the Portuguese king, Sebastian, was defeated and killed in a battle with the Moors in Morocco. For two years Portugal was now ruled by the mad Cardinal Henry. On the latter's death Philip II of Spain seized the kingdom of Portugal; and for sixty years these two rivals for the trade of West Africa remained united under one crown - an unwilling and therefore not always close union.

The French and English were not slow to test the effect of this union on their chances of capturing more of the West African trade. An exiled and bankrupt pretender to the Portuguese throne 'sold' to some London and Devon merchants the monopoly of trade with the Gambia. In 1588 Elizabeth I sanctioned the 'sale', but ten years later transferred the claim to the Earl of Nottingham and Sir John Stanhope. The French promptly challenged these English claims, and eventually succeeded in establishing strong trading positions for themselves to the north of the Gambia River; whilst the English, as we have seen, were establishing themselves on that river itself and to the south. Both English and French achieved these successes at the expense of the insecurely balanced Portuguese-Spanish crown.

The fact that this crown was reluctantly shared by the two kingdoms was only one reason for these English and French successes. The other was that the Spaniards and Portuguese had become more interested in the New World, first brought to their knowledge a century before this by Christopher Columbus, than in the interloper-ridden Guinea coast. They were investing more and more of their capital in the plantations of the West Indies and the Spanish Main, and were becoming readier to buy the slaves they needed for these plantations from such 'interlopers' as John Hawkins.

b. SIERRA LEONE

The fort built by the Portuguese on Tombo Island on the Sierra Leone River between 1482 and 1495, and the trading base they set up at Port Loko at about the same time, may have led you to expect that the Portuguese were to become well established on the coast of modern Sierra Leone by the beginning of the sixteenth century. This, however, was not to be the case. Portuguese interest in Sierra Leone - or 'Serra Lyoa' as they called it - declined throughout the century, whereas Portuguese interest in the Gambia and the Mina coast (part of modern Ghana) remained high during the first half of the century at least. Sierra Leone was throughout this century an arena for the tangled rivalries of private interlopers.

These rivalries were fought out against a picturesque back ground. A Portuguese trader on the Sierra Leone River at the beginning of this century gave a sketchy picture of the country and people, especially of Pymto, a mountain village which gave its name to the whole mountainous peninsula at this time. The Bullom people who lived along this part of the coast had several other villages near enough to the shore to be regularly visited by the Portuguese traders — Manguy, Maguem and Bop. We know from another citizen of Lisbon, Pacheco Pereira, who was to become Governor of Elmina, that Temne as well as Bullom (or Sherbro) lived on or near the estuary of the Sierra Leone River at this time; for Pereira gives us some Temne as well as Sherbro words. He formed the impression of a wild, untamed land, and says it was this characteristic (rather than the peal of thunder or the shape of the mountains, see page 81) which led da Sintra to give it its name. It must also have been attractive or lucrative, or both - as early as 1513 some Portuguese had made their homes on this peninsula.

Living side by side, certainly not in peace, but at least without any major inter-state upheavals, Loko, Bullom and Temne learnt during the first half of the century to trade with Portuguese, Spanish and French. William and John Hawkins, whom we have already met in this chapter, called regularly at the anchorage da Sintra's men had discovered (page 81). The Portuguese, in spite of their waning interest, left a bold mark on place names in the area - the Sulima River was for centuries known as the Rio di li Fuimi (Smoke River); the Kife River as the Rio das Galinhas (River of Fowls); and the Mano River as the Rio des Monos (River of Monkeys). Portuguese caravels traded in the Waanje River, and sailed seventy miles up it to Mano Bonjema, leaving behind tinware in exchange for slaves.

But this relatively peaceful existence was disturbed soon after the middle of the century. A small but warlike people from the kingdom of Quoja on Cape Mount (called by the Portuguese Capo del Monte) known as the Mani began to move north-westwards along the coast in 1561, led by their kings, Sasina and Seterama. The Mani were polygamous and pagan, armed with bows and borne in canoes. It is possible that they were seeking refuge from the all-conquering Askia Mohammed of Songhai, whom we learnt about in Chapter 5, and of whom they had perhaps at some earlier stage been vassals. The Loko, Bullom and Temne kings along the Sierra Leone River hurriedly joined forces against the invaders, whilst the European slavers circled like impatient vultures, waiting to benefit richly from the expected bloodshed. First the Bullom, whose king, Farma, had his chief town at Tagrin, then the Temne, were defeated by the Mani. The Limba and Yalunka, by employing scorched-earth and guerilla tactics, were able to delay the Mani for longer. But the latter swept up the Scarcies River, digging up and selling the gold ornaments buried with the dead nobles, and secured the help of the Portuguese in an attack on the Susu and Fulani. The latter however had cavalry, and this proved to be the Mani's undoing. They were defeated at last at the end of the century. Unable or unwilling to return to Cape Mount, they remained in what is today Sierra Leone, some providing for many years ruling families for the Loko, others intermarrying with Temne and Bullom, and yet others inhabiting some parts of what is today Mende country.

The European slave traders took swift advantage of all this disturbance. Sierra Leone was well known as a good harbour and a place where water supplies could be obtained, and also a good source of fresh fruit and fish (particularly the Sherbro area). Now the Mani wars had for the time being created in addition a plentiful supply of slaves in the form of prisoners of war taken by one side or the other.

So as the century closes we are left by the writers of the period with an impression of a land as commercially attractive as it was picturesque. Alvares d'Almada, a Portuguese from Cape Verde, writing in 1594, describes the natural products of Sierra Leone as 'abundant'. He says these included cotton, ivory, wax, gold, amber, pepper, sugar, iron and wood. He mentions the great advantages offered to ships bound for the Indies by the natural harbour on the southern side of the estuary of the river, and that many Portuguese from Santiago in the Cape Verde Islands wanted to migrate to Sierra Leone. The people of Sierra Leone he tells us had a judiciary, with the king presiding as judge over a court called a 'funco', assisted by elders called 'solategi', and with advocates in masks, plumes and bells appearing before him. Convicted sorcerers were immediately executed by the lances carried by attendants. The elders were chosen by the king to advise him on matters of state as well as points of law, and paid out of fines levied by the court in which they sat. The king succeeded his father or brother; and whereas elders were ceremonially smeared with goat's blood and rice flour on appointment, the king on his accession was bathed, bound, toughened by being put through various ordeals, then regally clothed and given a staff called a 'queto'. When he went out in procession with his elders everyone else had to keep indoors; and on his death he, with his gold, was buried outside the village, a hut being erected later over his grave, whilst other corpses, also with their gold, were buried in their own compounds. D'Almada also refers to the women's secret societies which kept young girls apart from the rest of the community for a year or more, after which they emerged to dance and display their beauty before their suitors. This writer says the name of that society was 'menda'. We are tempted at once to see a similarity between it and the 'bundu' society of modern times; but we must remember that many of the customs d'Almada describes at the end of the sixteenth century are to be found in very similar form in many parts of West Africa today, and many of them have been noted by us in some of the pre-European empires of West Africa already studied. It is much safer to say that the people d'Almada was describing were a typical negro people of West Africa, than to try to identify them with any particular modern people. For the writer himself merely describes them as the people of 'Serra Lyoa'.

However, his account proved sufficiently convincing to lead Philip III of Spain to send to Sierra Leone its first Christian missionary. He was sixty-seven-year-old Balthazar Barreira, a Jesuit and close friend of the king. Barreira arrived in 1605, and a year later was celebrating mass, fittingly, on Tombo Island - the site, you will remember, of the first, short- lived Portuguese fort in this area.[1] He also set up a church on the south shore of the estuary, probably near the modern Kroo Bay: but when he tried to make converts up the Scarcies River he found the Muslims there in strength before him, and had to withdraw.

c. THE GOLD COAST

The vulnerable fort built by the Portuguese during the fifteenth century at Elmina and named São Jorge da Mina (page 82) was only the first of many similar structures to be erected by the Europeans on the coast of modern Ghana. In 1503 the Portuguese built a fort at Axim to control the movement of gold from Denkyera to the coast. In 1526 they built a similar fort at Shama, and in 1576 one at Accra. All these were placed under the authority of the Governor of Elmina, who in the 1520s was the Pacheco Pereira to whom I have already referred (page 91).

But even whilst they were building more forts on this coast, the Portuguese were turning their attention increasingly to the other side of the Atlantic (page 90). It is true that Pereira was reprimanded by his royal masters when he disclosed, in his writing and talking, too many useful geographical and navigational details about the Guinea coast. But no amount of secrecy could save a monopoly which had already been so extensively breached. Between 1500 and

---

[1] P. 82

1503 the French alone captured 300 Portuguese caravels on this coast. In 1507 we know that between Efutu and the Volta the Portuguese hardly did any trade, and it was left to interlopers to open up that stretch of the coast later.

Before about 1550 the French were easily the most active of these interlopers; but from about that date onwards the English appeared off this coast in increasing numbers. Just as in 1492 a Portuguese rebel had been found in command of a French privateer (page 83), so in 1553 a Portuguese captain called Antonio Pinteado brought a convoy of four ships owned by one Thomas Windham of Portsmouth to Elmina, where they bought 150 lb. of gold. They then went on to Benin in search of pepper. There ill health befell them, and Pinteado and Windham died, with ninety-eight others. However, the amount of gold brought back to England by the surviving forty sailors was so great that this voyage encouraged rather than deterred other sea-dogs.

In 1554 another English merchant, John Lok, took a fleet to Shama; and it is interesting to note that the interlopers were now operating in fleets instead of singly. He fought a brief battle with the Portuguese fort there, then sailed on to Cape Coast, where he traded without any opposition. The same thing happened at Kormantine and Beraku. He then returned to Shama, which he now found deserted. He took the opportunity to secure some gold here; but it cost him the lives of twenty- four men struck down by illness. Yet another English merchant, William Towerson, made similar voyages in 1555, 1556 and 1558, on the first of these allying successfully with French interlopers against the Portuguese.

It was about now that the English interlopers realized the advantages of a permanent association to promote trade in Guinea, instead of temporary associations such as that formed between Windham and Pinteado in 1553, and that formed between Towerson and his French counterparts in 1555. In 1561 'The Company of Merchant Adventurers for Guinea' was formed in London. The people of the coast near Elmina could not have fully sensed that the new company represented, in addition to an opportunity for extended trade, a threat to their sovereignty and way of life. However, in 1570 the Comani and Fetu people joined together to make the most determined assault Elmina Castle was to suffer whilst in Portuguese hands. The assault failed; but it proves that at a very early stage of European contact with the people of the Guinea coast the ill effects on these people of this contact were at least partly realized by them, side by side with the trading advantages which it brought. One reason for the failure of this assault was the new watch-tower which the Portuguese had built in the fort in 1556. This watch-tower is today probably encased in the relatively new tower over the entrance to the courtyard of the modern castle. If this is so, it is the oldest structure in West Africa which has remained in continuous use.

Towards the end of the century a new nation joined the ranks of challengers to the now very weak Portuguese claims of monopoly over the trade of this coast. After the conquest of Portugal by Philip II of Spain in 1580 (page 90), Dutch rebels, whose country was at the time a Spanish possession, launched a series of attacks on Portuguese and Spanish posts in Africa and America. In 1595 the first Dutch voyage was made to the Gold Coast. So weak was the Portuguese hold on the trade of this coast by this time that the Dutch were able in 1598 to establish two small fortified factories on each side of Elmina, at Butri, Kormantine, Mori and Kommenda; and to start a profitable trade through these posts.

d. THE SLAVE COAST

If the coast of modern Ghana was famous in the sixteenth century for the gold it produced, that of modern Nigeria had the much less happy reputation of being the most profitable source of slaves of any section of the West African coast. The Rio dos Esclavos to which I have already referred (page 84) was the centre of this trade; but there must have been very many places in this region where an unscrupulous European trader could fill his holds with slaves, in exchange for the familiar cheap European commodities which elsewhere along the coast he was more likely to trade for ivory or gold. We know that, between 1530 and 1660, 900,000 slaves were shipped across the Atlantic by the Portuguese alone. When you take into account the slave trade by other nations and in other years, the total transported towards the New World from West Africa (between 1500 and 1864) is reckoned to have been about 20,000,000. Indeed, as early as 1600 there were almost certainly more negroes in the West Indies than natives, and even today the majority of the population of the state of Bahia in the republic of Brazil are of negro descent and retain strong traces of Yoruba culture.

The majority of these slaves came from the coast of modern Nigeria. By 1500, when Fernao de Mello became Captain of São Tomé, slaves were already being carried from Benin through São Tomó to Elmina, from where they were taken to Portugal. In 1502 the Spaniard Nicolas de Ovando took the first slaves across the Atlantic to work on the new plantations of the New World. They were so useful to the planters there that in 1510 the use of negro slaves in the New World was extended to the gold mines of Hispaniola, to which 250 such slaves were sent by the Spaniards. Soon, however, the Spaniards found it more convenient to sell to other nations the right of supplying negro slaves to their American and Caribbean mines and plantations. This right, known as the 'Asiento', went first to the Portuguese, and then (in 1713, by the Treaty of Utrecht), to the British.

Not all of the slaves who were taken away from the Slave Coast, either after being stolen or after being bought, actually left West Africa. The settlers of São Tomé had increasing trading links with the mainland during the sixteenth century, and brought to the island some of the slaves from Benin. These slaves worked on the extensive and very lucrative sugar plantations established by de

Mello on the island. With the slaves from Benin to São Tomé came pepper, which was highly valued by the Europeans. I have referred to Windham's ill-fated journey to Benin in search of that commodity.[1] He seems to have been surprised to find that the king there could speak Portuguese fluently.

The Gwato factory we noted (page 85) as having been built by the Portuguese near the mouth of the Benin River was visited by both missionaries and traders from Portugal in the early years of this century. The missionaries made another unsuccessful attempt to convert the King of Gwato to Christianity, though they may have made converts of some of his princes and nobles. The traders remained in Gwato from 1486 to about 1520, soon after which it was finally abandoned. The link with Portugal did remain, however, and in 1540 the King of Benin sent an ambassador to pay a visit to the Portuguese capital. The Portuguese described the Benin capital at this time as having a nine-mile wall round it. English traders calling at Benin during this century record having obtained there 'pepper and elephants' teeth, oil of palm, cloth made of cotton wool very curiously woven, and cloth made of the bark of palm trees' by people who 'are very gentle and loving' and who used white cowrie shell as currency.

---

[1] P. 95

11

The Seventeenth Century —
Companies and Castles

a. SENEGAMBIA

T he weakening of Spanish-Portuguese influence in West Africa which we noted in the previous chapter continued during the early part of the seventeenth century. In addition to the English, French and Dutch to whom I have already referred, Danes and Germans now appeared as traders on this coast.

In 1612 the French tried to erect a fort on the Gambia River. Unfortunately for them, they started the work during the rains, and ill health forced them to abandon it. Five years later the Dutch States-General (Parliament) established a West India Company to trade between Europe, Africa and America, and by 1621 this company had set up a factory on Goree Island, ninety miles north of the Gambia estuary. In 1618 there was formed the second noteworthy English company trading on this coast — successor to the Company of Merchant Adventurers for Guinea of 1561 (page 94). This new company was called 'The Company of Adventurers of London Trading to Guinea and Benin'. The main commodity in which this company traded was redwood, and it had bought its patent (i.e. exclusive trading rights) from James I.

In addition to the companies, many English, French and Dutch pirates operated off this coast, using violent methods of acquiring wealth. And when the Dutch and English companies' ships had safely avoided or beaten off the pirates there were still the Portuguese 'monopolists' to be reckoned with. The new English company's first expedition was that of a single ship called the *Catherine* to the Gambia, and it was promptly destroyed by Portuguese attackers. The next ship to be sent out by this company, the *St John,* was better armed, and survived both pirate and Portuguese hostility. Her captain, however, relied on the large supply of alcohol he carried to gain influence and make friends with the people of the Gambia, but did not adequately protect this supply from his own crew. As a result, many of his sailors became useless to him through excessive drinking, and he had to return home, the company losing £6,000.

The Dutch alone are known to have had forty ships in the West African trade in 1622. In addition, most of these sea-faring European countries had some of their citizens engaged purely in exploration on the coast. The Englishman Richard Jobson, for example, actually refused a cargo-load of slaves offered him by Gambian chiefs in 1620, saying he had come to explore, and in any case disapproved of the slave trade.

By 1629 the Company of Adventurers had failed, not surprisingly. The French merchants of Rouen had also set up a Guinea trading company by now, whose factors were mainly interested in the Senegal gum trade; and in that year they seized in the Gambia one of the ships of the collapsing English company. The following year a new English company was formed - 'The Company of Merchants Trading to Guinea' - and was given a patent by Charles I. In 1633 Richelieu retaliated by giving the French company, known after 1681 as 'The Senegal Company', a monopoly of trade between the Senegal and the Gambia for thirty years. It was this company which built the fort of St Louis on an island at the mouth of the Senegal.

Meanwhile the Dutch West India Company, formed in 1617, was equally busy. Between 1627 and 1636 it sent a number of ships to the Gambia to trade, which they did with some success. In 1638 the Dutch company succeeded in capturing the Portuguese fort at Arguin, and held it for forty years, when the French seized it. The contribution of the Spanish to the history of the Gambia during this period seems to have been mainly religious: in 1647 twelve Capuchin monks from Spain landed in the area to start missionary work.

In 1651 yet another English trading company was formed, 'The Company of London Merchants'. It launched one disastrous Gambian voyage and then concentrated on the Sherbro area of Sierra Leone and the Kormantine area of the Gold Coast; thus the Gambia trade was more than ever open to the ships of trading companies from the continent of Europe and of interlopers and pirates from all nations. When, however, Puritans fell from power in England and the Stuarts were restored (1660), the new king, Charles II, learnt from his cousin Prince Rupert of the great wealth supposedly obtained by the Dutch from the Gambia. Charles now formed one of the most famous of English trading companies of this century, the 'Royal Adventurers of England Trading into Africa'. It traded in gold, redwood and slaves. The gold was believed to come from a mountain near the source of the River Gambia, the redwood from the banks of that river and the slaves from the Gold and Slave Coasts. A monopoly was claimed for the Company in the Gambia. This was backed up by the seizure from the Duke of Courland (a Baltic province of Sweden) of St Andrews Island, which one of the Duke's sailors, a private adventurer, had seized some years before and 'presented' to the Duke. The island was now renamed 'James Island' in honour of the Duke of York, who had a large financial interest in the new company. The king's name was strangely perpetuated: Dog Island was seized and renamed Charles Island. The Company promised to allow the Courlanders to trade in the Gambia, but did not keep this promise.

The French soon sought to match the success of the 'Royal Adventurers'. Between 1664 and 1674 a French East India Company and a French West India Company were set up, and the latter carried slaves from the Guinea coast to the French West Indian plantations on Martinique and Guadeloupe, a trade formerly in the Dutch company's hands. The English replied by forming in 1668 'The Company of Gambia Adventurers', to whom the 'Royal Adventurers' sub-let their 'monopoly' in the Gambia. This was at least a four-sided struggle, however: the Dutch company still held their forts at Arguin and Goree, and the Portuguese a foothold on the Bintang Creek up the

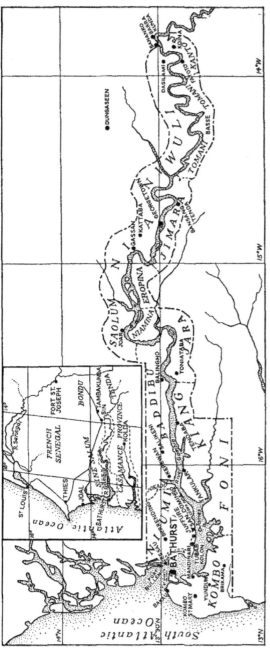

Map 10 Senegambia and Gambia

Gambia River.

This was the period of frequent Anglo-Dutch conflict in Europe and at sea; and the effect was felt in West Africa in frequent capturing and recapturing of the European forts there. In 1664 alone Goree passed from Dutch to English, and then back to Dutch hands, and James Fort (Gambia) was destroyed by the Dutch. The disturbed conditions also affected trade. Charles Island was abandoned by the 'Gambia Adventurers', who also lost both slaves and employees in a serious revolt of slaves on James Island in 1667. In 1674 the French West India Company was dissolved, and the older French company, the Senegal Company, was revived by Colbert. This seized in 1677 the fort at Goree which the Dutch had held for fifty-six years (with the exception of the brief British tenure we have just noted), and the Dutch West India Company in turn collapsed, at least so far as its interest in West Africa was concerned.

On the whole the English by this time seemed to be making most profit from the trade of the Gambia. When the 'Royal Adventurers' were succeeded in 1672 by the 'Royal African Company', the new company ended the sub-lease of the 'Gambia Adventurers', and took over itself the thriving trade in redwood in the area. Before 1678 the Dutch had been the chief rivals of the English. The French now succeeded to this position; in 1681 they began paying a local king rent for a factory at Albreda opposite James Island.

There were still many perils, as well as much wealth, to be found by Europeans in the Gambia. Of these perils, the most feared was illness. At the beginning of 1662, of the 119 employees of the 'Gambia Adventurers' on Charles Island, only forty-seven were at one time fit for duty. In eight months between 1683 and 1684 twenty-two of the Royal African Company's servants died of ill health. Yet still others came, undaunted; for the Gambia alone was at this time said to yield 500 to 600 slaves a year, fourteen to fifteen tons of ivory, the same weight of wax and - a new item, this - 10,000 hides.

Gradually towards the end of this century the French strength on the Gambia grew. They made increasing use of their lease at Albreda. When their only building there was burnt down in 1686 they erected five in its place and one more at Geregia. We cannot be sure whether the Royal African Company did not wish to interfere, or was not able to do so. In any case, more than a century of alternating peace and war lay ahead for England, not this time with Holland, but with France. Soon after the first of these wars, the War of the English Succession, broke out, the Royal African Company reduced its staff in Sierra Leone in order to strengthen its staff on James Island - a move which reveals the relative value of the two 'possessions'. The English destroyed Albreda and Geregia and from 1692 to 1693 the French forts at Senegal and Goree were in English hands. On the other hand the English fort on James Island was destroyed by the French in 1695, and not rebuilt by the English until an uneasy peace was made at Ryswick in 1698. The French did not attempt to rebuild Albreda and Geregia.

Right at the end of the century we find that for the first time the right of any company to claim or be given a monopoly of the trade of a particular region was successfully challenged at Westminster by interests representing the interlopers. The English Revolution of 1688 had brought into Parliament politicians less tied to the old commercial interests than their predecessors. Cloth manufacturers, who used the dye made from Gambia and Sherbro redwood, complained that this cost up to £90 more per ton than it needed to do, as a result of the Company's monopoly. The new politicians therefore attacked this monopoly with determination. Finally in 1698 an Act was passed which opened the trade of Africa to all, but required private traders to pay the Company a 10 per cent duty on their imports to help meet the cost of maintaining the forts.

The Company could, of course, still trade, and did so. But the now legal and respectable interlopers, or '10-per-cent men' as they came to be known, very quickly exploited their new advantage. In six months alone, in 1698, English interlopers are estimated to have transported 3,600 slaves across the Atlantic. In addition there were of course other interlopers, from whom it was not possible to collect the 10 per cent duty. But although the Company's factory on James Island was rebuilt, the days of the trading companies were numbered, especially as gold and slaves were exempt from this duty. Besides most of the '10-per-cent men' were in the rapidly growing ports of Bristol and Liverpool, whilst the Company's interests were practically all confined to one port, London.

b. SIERRA LEONE

At the beginning of the seventeenth century the Sierra Leone peoples in contact with the Europeans were the Loko, Susu and Limba in the north, and the Temne, Bullom and Mani in the south. The Loko were losing their previously dominant position in the area, and for a short while during this century even their capital, Port Loko, was in the hands of the Temne. The European nations with whom these peoples had most dealings were England, France, Holland, Portugal and Spain. The arrival of the Spanish Jesuit Balthazar Barreira on Tombo Island has already been referred to (page 93). Although he left Sierra Leone in 1609, having failed to make any converts in the Scarcies, he did succeed in baptizing (though not necessarily converting) a number of kings on the Sierra Leone River, and in building some wooden churches. He accused the Europeans in Sierra Leone of living like heathens, but nevertheless helped them to acquire a site for a fort - an early example, often to be repeated, of collaboration between missionary and trader. This site was offered to Philip III of Spain in 1606 by King Felipe, the ruler of the southern bank of the mouth of the Sierra Leone River, and was at the modern Kroo Bay. A contract was let by the Spanish for the erection of the fort, but French rivals defrauded the contractor of all his goods and ships.

The Portuguese had a very small share of the trade of Sierra Leone during this century, very few of their ships ever calling there then, although Sierra Leone was only twenty days' sailing from Lisbon. Dutch interests here were growing, however. They established bases during this century in Gallinas, Cape Mount and Robaga. However, Felipe, threatened by Philip III with the loss of Spanish-Portuguese trade, would not allow the Dutch to build a fort on his territory, which included the valuable watering place now known as King Jimmy. If they could not obtain water easily, however, the Dutch seem to have had little difficulty with gold. A report to Philip III by a Spaniard named Bartholomew André in 1606 states that the Dutch carried away 2,000 lb. of gold ornaments a year from Sierra Leone, many of them dug up from the graves of kings and nobles. Sugar cane, cotton, timber, tow (used for sealing ships' bottoms), gum, oil-seeds and redwood are listed as other products available here at this time. The Dutch base at Gallinas was abandoned in 1640, but in 1669 there were still eight or ten Dutchmen at Robaga.

The French were equally active. They had a fort at Bure on the south bank of the Sierra Leone River, near Gambia Island, and, as we have seen, they were strong enough to prevent the Spanish from erecting a fort on King Felipe's territory. The French regarded the Spanish and Portuguese as their main rivals here, and on at least one occasion this attitude was justified: in 1619 the Portuguese killed the entire crew of a French barque seven or eight leagues above the residence of the King of Tagrin.

James Barbot, Agent-General of the French Royal Company of Africa, tells us how King Fatima of Bullom had several subject rulers, some of whom, like one 'Dom Miguel', had been baptized by Barreira and had adopted a Christian name. Fatima and his successors were styled 'Kings of Bullom' by the French, whilst Felipe was King of Bourre, and the Sierra Leone River was known as the Mitombo. A Capuchin priest called Seraphim was continuing the missionary work of Barreira in the north in the 1640s, building churches in Port Loko and Tombo; but ill health caused the closing of this mission thirty years later.

But the biggest traders hereabouts were probably still the English. In 1607, for example, a certain William Keeling put into the Sierra Leone River in search, not of trade, but of water and refuge from storms. Yet he was able to leave it with gold ornaments, a 63-lb. tusk and several thousand limes, essential to prevent crews from developing scurvy during the long voyages. Although Bartholomew André and Balthazar Barreira could not have been very far away, Keeling says he saw no other Europeans when he landed at the watering place. He did, however find carved on a stone the names of Drake and Fenton; and added his own.

P. 11 The Sultan of Bornu receiving an English mission

P. 12 King Jaja of Opobo

P. 13 King Akitoye of Lagos listening to James White preaching

P. 14 Christiansborg Castle

P. 15 Fort St. Iago

The newly formed Company of London Merchants (page 98) built factories in Sherbro from 1651 onwards, and the Navigation Acts of the English Parliaments helped the English traders greatly in their rivalry with other Europeans. Ten years later the new Royal Adventurers' Company (page 98) was also trading in Sierra Leone, using a ship captained by an enterprising sailor named Holmes. He erected a fort on Tasso Island, and sub-let part of the trade of the area to private traders - thus foreshadowing the 10 per cent agreement made thirty years later. The 'Royal Adventurers' went on to build at Bunce the first English factory on the Sierra Leone River, and to take over in 1663 the Sherbro factories which the Company of London Merchants had handed to the East India Company in 1657 for five years; but the 'Royal Adventurers' were themselves liquidated in 1671. The Sierra Leone forts, together with those on the Gambia and the Gold Coast, were then acquired by the new Royal African Company for a total of £34,000. The Tasso Island fort had by then been destroyed by the Dutch admiral, de Ruyter (1664).

The picture we are left with of the people of Sierra Leone towards the end of the seventeenth century is of a people living in relative peace and happiness in their attractive setting. On the north bank of the great estuary was the fertile low-lying Bullom land, with its own king and its missionaries. A little way up the estuary itself were the numerous islands such as Gambia, Tasso and Bunce on which the European traders were erecting their forts. You can still visit today the ruins of the fort on Bunce Island. On the south bank were the massed hills streaked with tenuous waterfalls during the rains, and its good anchorage, good water and plentiful limes. Still farther south was the Sherbro country with its river navigable by sea-going ships for twenty leagues, as far as Baga, where the English had their factory; and offering a plentiful supply of camwood, as well as food such as rice, maize, bananas, sweet potatoes, sugar cane, plantains, figs, pineapples, lemons, oranges, pumpkins, water melons, cola nuts and fowls. Both on Sherbro Island and on the mainland the people were described as wearing striped calico. The villages were well populated, and amongst the unpretentious houses of Baga was a large hall where ceremonies were held and visitors welcomed.

Bunce Island, Sierra Leone's best-known historical site, was first fortified by the Royal African Company which had been founded in 1672 (page 100). This company also established a fort on York Island to the south. It abandoned York in 1726 and Bunce in 1728; but before then its initial capital of £100,000 had produced profits running into many millions of pounds. The main trading commodities were brass and pewter utensils, iron bars, cloth and muskets on the one hand, and camwood, ivory and slaves on the other. The underground chambers into which slaves were crowded whilst awaiting shipment may still be seen in the Bunce fort.

However, during the closing years of the seventeenth century it is clear that trade on the Sierra Leone River was on the decline. The Portuguese were doing better in their two small remaining posts at Cacheo and on the Scarcies than were the English on Bunce and Sherbro. The reason was probably the growing strength of the interlopers, which led to the ending of the Company's monopoly in 1698 which we have noted (page 101). In 1683 a French pirate named Jean Hamlin captured no fewer than seventeen English and Dutch ships in the Sierra Leone River. Two years later a warehouse at Bunce was destroyed by fire, with heavy loss. In 1687 the Bunce factor, John Case, was robbed of his stock of ivory by a Dutch pirate; the following year the Sherbro factory had to be abandoned so as to strengthen the York one, whilst at Bunce, Case and four of the Company's vessels were taken by a French interloper. In 1695 Bunce was again attacked and sacked by the French.

However, much of the blame for this state of affairs must rest with the Company's servants, who were frequently disloyal to it. They allowed interlopers and middlemen to trade amongst them, and pocketed many of the profits which should have gone to the Company. Sometimes they then deserted its service and turned interloper themselves.

Finally in this century we must note the advancing power of the Temne in Sierra Leone. At the start of the century the great Mani people were still overlords of Bullom, Loko and Temne, and the Mani emperor, Turay, claimed the allegiance of the peoples of much of the coastline, even though the Mani themselves, small in number, did not often come into contact with the Europeans. But then Turay's family intermarried with the ruling families of the Bullom, such as that of Fatima, and the Mani line would have disappeared when he died in 1610 had not Felipe, son of Farima, a relative and subject of Turay's, who ruled the Loko from Rotumba, deliberately kept Mani blood pure a little longer. It was this Felipe who eventually inherited Turay's kingdom, with the exception of the Loko country, which went to one of Turay's zons.

Mani power was now, like Loko, clearly on the decline. To try to halt the decline, Felipe allied with a little-known people called the Sapi or Capeo[1] who had formed a federation of peoples in the interior of Sierra Leone in this century, apparently to oppose the Limba and Susu. But the people who were really on the move were the Temne, who at the end of the century had advanced right into the Sierra Leone peninsula and split the Bullom into a northern group, who live on the shore which still bears their name, and a southern group, the modern Sherbro.

---

[1] P. 81

c. THE GOLD COAST

The trading companies we have seen active on the Gambia and Sierra Leone rivers in the seventeenth century also operated profitably on the Gold Coast in very similar circumstances and with very similar commodities. The Portuguese concentrated on gold mining at Elmina, and only transferred some of their efforts to Aowin on the Ankobra River in 1623 after some of the tunnelling at Elmina had collapsed and the workers had gone on strike. At once it became clear that the people of the area resented any extension of European influence or claims as far inland as Aowin, which was fifteen miles upstream. The Portuguese forts were attacked both here and at Elmina in 1624-5, although without much success. Finally in 1636 another collapse of the Elmina workings brought a more determined and successful attack. When a Dutch attack followed the native one, the Portuguese abandoned Elmina and fled to Axim (1637).

The Dutch had their main centre at Mori, from which in 1625 they had attacked, unsuccessfully, the Portuguese at Elmina, using 1,200 men, including many natives. Twenty years later we read of the Dutch having 130 European traders still on the Guinea coast, most of them at the enlarged fort at Mori; but their success against the Portuguese at Elmina in 1637 was due as much to their occupation of the dominating nearby hill of St. Iago as to their numerical strength. They now built Fort Iago (or Conraadsborg) on this hill, and followed the retreating Portuguese to Axim. This they captured in 1642, forcing the Portuguese finally out of the western end of the Gold Coast. By the middle of this century, the Portuguese had only precarious footholds in Guinea at Cacheo, on the Scarcies, and later for a brief period at Christiansborg, whilst the Dutch were rivalling the English as the most powerful trading nation there. The Portuguese were however at this time more interested in developing their colony in Brazil than in their trade in West Africa. The Dutch had given up all claims on Brazil in return for a Portuguese surrender of claims to the Gold Coast. At this point where the Portuguese leave the Gold Coast it should be noted that to the Portuguese is owed the introduction of many of the agricultural products on which not only the Gold Coast but also all West Africa depend - citrus fruits, rice, the sugar cane, cassava, maize, guava, tobacco, pineapple, yams - some from the Far East and some from America. They also brought cattle to the coastal regions, and left a number of Portuguese words which in the course of time were absorbed into the trading language of the Guinea coast.

The English Company of London Merchants formed in 1651 was specially charged, amongst other things, with the responsibility of trading in the Cormantine area. All the forts owned by this company on the Gold Coast were acquired by the East India Company in 1657, the 'Royal Adventurers' in 1662 and the Royal African Company in 1672. There was an attack by the people of Elmina on the Dutch Fort (St Iago), in 1681; and then the English, like the Dutch before them, tried to seize what they hoped was a weakened garrison. But Elmina was in fact stronger now than ever before, and they failed on this occasion, and on another exactly a century later (1781); finally succeeding in acquiring Elmina by purchase only in 1872. The English headquarters remained at Cape Coast throughout this period.

But the English were not the only Europeans attacking the rapidly growing Dutch strength on the Gold Coast in the seventeenth century. Swedes, Danes, French and Germans all joined battle, against one another as well as the Dutch. The latter replaced their trading posts at Shama and Butri with forts, and built new factories at Accra, Anomabu and Kormantine. The Swedes established their factories at Takoradi, Cape Coast and Osu in the middle of the century; but in 1657, only five years after the last was completed, the Danes captured them all, and then went on to build another fort at Cape Coast (Amanfro) and to enlarge Osu, renaming it Christiansborg. They must have felt they were overstretching themselves, however; for in the 1670s they sold Amanfro to the English and abandoned Fort Witsen at Takoradi, which was also promptly acquired by the English.

During the Anglo-Dutch wars of this period, in fact, the Gold Coast forts changed hands with perplexing speed. During the ten years' existence of the 'Royal Adventurers' (1662-72), for example, we know that first Cape Coast and Egya were taken by the Dutch from the English, then recovered by the English Captain Holmes, who at the same time seized or acquired Takoradi, Shama, Mori and Anomabu from the Dutch (1664). The following year the great Dutch admiral, de Ruyter, regained them all except heavily defended Cape Coast, and Egya, which the English had destroyed. Moreover, de Ruyter succeeded in adding Winneba, Kormantine and Kommenda to his prizes.

It was this series of reverses which led to the collapse of the 'Royal Adventurers' in 1672. After the Treaty of Breda (1672) Cape Coast was the only Gold Coast fort they still held and could sell to the Royal African Company. This accounts for the low price (£34,000) the latter company paid for all its predecessors' forts (page 105).

The new company tackled its problems vigorously at first. It built James Fort in Accra, and built or rebuilt forts at Kommenda, Dixcove, Winneba, Sekondi and Anomabu. Trade both in gold and in slaves expanded on the Gold Coast. The Royal Mint struck its first gold 'guineas', and 300,000 slaves crossed the Atlantic in the holds of English ships during the last twenty years of the century, almost half of them carried by the Company, the rest by interlopers.

We may then summarize the state of the parties trading on the Gold Coast at the end of the seventeenth century. The Danes held only Christiansborg. The Portuguese flag had flown for three final years (1679-82) over Christiansborg but had now finally been run down on this coast. The Germans (called Brandenburgers before 1701, Prussians after) also held only one fort, at Cape

Three Points, and the French held one, at Kommenda. The English (whom we must now call the British, as they were joined both constitutionally and in their overseas adventures by the Scots) held six: Cape Coast, the apparently impregnable headquarters; Kommenda; Dixcove; Winneba; Sekondi; and Anomabu. The Dutch claims were the most numerous of all: to forts at Elmina (Conraadsborg, also sometimes referred to as St Iago); Accra; Axim; Butri; Mori; Sekondi; Takoradi; Kormantine; Shama; Beraku; Apam and Kommenda; twelve in all.

I have referred to the Europeans' 'claims' to the ownership of forts on the Gold Coast (and there are the remains of no fewer than thirty-two such forts in modern Ghana); and I would use the same noun of all the so-called European 'possessions' in West Africa. For before title to property can lawfully or reasonably be regarded as having passed, there must be both understanding of and consent to the transaction on the part of both parties. And that the people of the Gold Coast wanted the trade of the Europeans but not their permanent occupation of their land there is no doubt. When the effect of the half-understood 'treaties' the Europeans had persuaded local kings to thumb-print became clear, or when the Europeans' gunpowder ran short, or their numbers fell to the mosquito's bite, the people of the coast would make quite clear what they thought of the Europeans' claims. We have already noted in this section two attacks (in 1637 and 1681) by the people of Elmina on the forts there (page 107). There were hundreds of similar attacks during this century. The Dutch even resorted to what was to become a familiar tactic of colonial powers, 'divide and rule' - turning one community against another in order to keep both in subjection. In 1694, as a full-scale war was fought between the Dutch on the one hand, and the Fante, the people of Kommenda and the Asebu, on the other, the people of Elmina were bribed into supporting the Dutch. Even this did not save the Dutch from defeat; but it did leave deep-seated bitterness, particularly between the Elmina and the Fante, as we shall see later. The fort at Apam was built against fierce local opposition. No fewer than ten times, European forts were actually captured by native attack, in spite of the vast difference in fire-power between the two sides, and in spite also of the 'ground rent' (4 oz. of gold a month at Elmina, Cape Coast and Anomabu, 2 oz. at Accra) paid to the kings by the Europeans.

The worst thing the Europeans' arrival in West Africa had done, however, was not to dispossess, but to demoralize. That there had been fighting and warfare before this arrival no one would deny; but it had been part of the necessary struggle for survival, a struggle which breaks out on a far more spectacular and bloody scale in the World Wars which Europeans and European-descended peoples engage in from time to time than it ever does amongst Africans. The fighting the European traders took part in or touched off in seventeenth-century West Africa was sometimes between company and company, government and government, company and interloper, interloper and interloper, African and European, or African and African. But whoever was involved, this fighting was much more demoralizing than any earlier warfare in the area, not because it was on a larger scale, but because it was motivated by greed, not self-preservation. No loyalties survived it for long. The European's loyalty to his company and to his nation was just as vulnerable to greed as the African's to his family, state and race. Where the loyalty showed signs of being stronger than the greed, it was weakened with bribes (recorded quite shamelessly in the traders' ledgers) or alcohol.

What worried the Royal African Company most at the end of the seventeenth century, however, was the challenge from the interlopers, not any question of right or wrong. I have mentioned how English interlopers actually carried more slaves than the Company during the last two decades. The Company made an unsuccessful attempt to levy 40 per cent of the value of an interloper's cargo as a fee for permission to trade in West Africa. Finally it secured statutory authority from the English Parliament for the 10 per cent arrangement we have noted (page 101).

We have not had cause yet to refer to the mighty Asante nation in this account of the growing loss of sovereignty in the Gold Coast to Europeans. But it was in the middle of this century that an important reversal in the direction of the flow of trade took place in the area just north of what was to become the capital of that nation, a reversal which was to help that nation to expand. Near modern Wenchi, north-west of Kumasi, is the village of Begho. In the seventeenth century this was a settlement of Mande-speaking peoples from the Empire of Mali, and a collecting point for the gold to be sent north through Jenne. About 1650 the people of Begho realized that they could get a better price for their gold at Elmina on the coast than at Jenne inland; and a trade route was opened to the coast through Tafo and Adansi, a trade route which was soon to become very well trodden. This route was from time to time used by armies as well as traders. In about 1670 the Adansi marched north along it with muskets bought on the coast and a military organization taught them by Akwamu, and invaded Tafo. Later the Asante were to extend their rule both north and south along it; for it now linked the coast, through their country, with the desert.

d. THE SLAVE COAST

The seventeenth-century trading companies and interlopers we have seen active in the Gambia, Sierra Leone and the Gold Coast bought, sold and exchanged commodities with equal zest on the Slave Coast farther east. Benin was still the main centre. James I had 'given' to 'The Company of Adventurers of London' (page 97) a monopoly of trade on this part of the coast. And 'trade' here meant almost exclusively slaves, in this century, these proving so much more profitable than the pepper for which Benin had been famous in the previous century.

But then Benin itself was now a very different place from the rich cultural centre we saw in Chapter 8. It is true that Europeans still wrote very flatteringly about it. A seventeenth-century Dutchman recorded:

'Benin is as large as Haarlem and surrounded by a wall. It is made up of many magnificent dwellings, and has beautiful long square galleries. . . . The roof of the largest of these is supported on wooden pillars sheathed entirely in copper engraved with the record of battles. Everything is very clean. Most of the king's buildings are roofed with palm leaves....and every gable is decorated with a turret on which stand copper birds with outstretched wings, very artistically made.'

But the truth was that Benin, having reached the height of its power in the fifteenth and sixteenth centuries, was now in decline. Although its power still extended nominally to Ouidah and Lagos, it was not effective. And it can hardly be a coincidence that Benin's greatness began to fade in the same century as saw the growth of the European slave trade. A Dutch writer in 1703, Bosman, notes the 'ruins of half-remaining houses' in Benin.

The people of Benin are Bini; but most of the slaves were Yoruba. In 1637 the Dutch, having freed themselves from the Spanish, temporarily seized the Portuguese colony of Brazil; and throughout this century they used the supremacy they had established in the trade of West Africa to keep the Brazilian plantations supplied with slaves. In the following century the British and French were to capture the lead from the Dutch in this field; but for the time being the typical slave ship flew the flag of Holland and was bound from Gwato via São Tomé to Brazil. I have referred to the Yoruba culture still to be found in Brazil. Professor E. L. Lasebikan, a Yoruba on the staff of the University of Bahia's Centre de Estudos-Afro-Orientais, listed a large number of words in current use in Salvador, capital of Bahia, Brazil, which speak eloquently of the volume of the slave trade between these two areas, and of the power of survival of Yoruba culture. These words include 'acaraje' for what Yoruba know as 'akara', 'mocoto' and 'muqueca' for 'mukeke' - all names of foods prepared in similar ways in both countries. There is a priestess of the Yoruba god Shango in Salvador, and there are Egungun rites on the island of Itaparica across the bay from Bahia.

Other ports from which slaves were exported in this country were Brass (Nembe), New Calabar (Owome) and Bonny in Ijaw country.[1] James Barbot, who warned against the dangers of 'pitaw'[2] on the Gold Coast, recorded that the rate of exchange for a male slave in Bonny was thirteen iron bars, and nine for a female. These ports gradually expanded during this century into trading

---

[1] See map p. 58
[2] An intoxicating liquor made from corn.

communities much like the city states of Italy. But whereas Ijaw political traditions before the arrival of Europeans had been democratic, with all adult males playing some part in government, these new trading communities tended to become very aristocratic in their politics, the trading houses winning and keeping to themselves power in government as well as commerce. It is worth noting, however, in reply to those who say that the European slave trade was only an extension of a practice already widespread amongst Africans, that the slaves in an Ijaw aristocratic household in the seventeenth century were treated as in every respect a part of the family; and when a successor as head of the family was being elected, it was ability, not birth, that mattered. Slaves were sometimes elected heads of families.

Farther east there were the Efik settlements at the Cross River estuary, with the powerful Egbo secret society in control of their government; and north of them the Aro who, like the people of Onitsha still farther to the north, are Ibo with their own separate states, based on trade. In the same way Warri,[1] south of Benin, had outgrown its dependence on Benin by the end of the seventeenth century, and its king or Olu seems to have had as close connections with the Portuguese during this century as the Oba of Benin had in the previous one. In 1644 the Olu of Warri was recorded as descended partly from the Portuguese, and in 1682 as being married to a Portuguese.

Then directly to the west of Benin was the kingdom of Oyo, whose culture we saw in Chapter 8 was closely linked with that of Benin and Ife. In this century the kingdom of Oyo was not yet in close contact with Europeans (who knew it only as the kingdom of Katunga) and so was saved the worst effects of the slave trade. Its people included the Yoruba, Egba, Ekiti and Ijebu, and it had a feudal emperor called Alafin elected from the Oyo Mesi or hereditary council of state. The Alafin's dominions were bounded by the Niger to the north, Benin to the east, the coastal marshes to the south, and, to the west, by Dahomey, an inland state founded in about 1625, with its capital at Abomey. Ojigi, the twelfth Alafin to rule from Oyo, attacked and crushed Porto Novo, capital of the coastal kingdom of Great Ardra, which was subject to Dahomey (1698).

The great states of Bornu and Kanem have a better recorded seventeenth-century history; but as the record is Arabic and not European it has been summarized in Chapter 6. We need only note here that when the Empire of Songhai received its death blow from the Moors, in 1591, the field was left clear for the rise of the power of Bornu under Mai Idris Alooma, who used his powerful army to unify the country and subdued its rebellious dependency Kanem before his death in 1617. Again we find interesting instances, as with the Ijaw to the south, of slaves in Bornu becoming rulers (of provinces in this case, not houses), if they had the necessary merit. It was external attacks by the Tuareg

---

[1] |See map p. 58

n the north and the Jukun in the south, not the internal demoralization of the European slave trade, which began to sap the strength of Bornu in the second half of the seventeenth century, when Mai Ali reigned (1657-94).

The Jukun of Kororofa on the Benue, whose king is known as the Aku, are cousins of the Kanuri, and had probably during the second half of the seventeenth century the most powerful state after Bornu in the north of what is today Nigeria. They had subjected Zaria in the previous century; in 1653 they attacked Kano, in 1671 Kano and Katsina, and in 1680 Bornu. The last-named attack was unsuccessful; and as the seventeenth century draws to a close, Bornu, although weaker, is still supreme in the belt of savannah country to the north of the Slave Coast.

12

The Eighteenth Century —Slaves and Factories

a. SENEGAMBIA

In West Africa during the eighteenth century we find some of the trends we noted during the previous century continuing, others being reversed. We also find a number of new trends appearing. The slave trade reached its peak during this century, but Britain and France, who were frequently at war replaced Holland as the biggest traders, as Holland had replaced Portugal and Spain during the previous century. The general contagion of treachery, vice and debauchery which the European slave trade had brought to West Africa grew worse, and the control exercised by our peoples over their own affairs, our sovereignty as we have called it, shrank still further. It was soon to be threatened not by European companies, but by European governments.

You will recall how during one of the Anglo-Dutch wars of the previous century an English captain called Holmes had captured from the Dutch a number of the forts originally built on the Gold Coast by the Company of Royal Adventurers (page 108). Holmes however was in the service, not of the Company, but of the government; and his great rival Admiral de Ruyter, who shortly after recovered these forts, similarly served his government. These incidents foreshadowed first the championing, and later the replacing, of commercial interests in West Africa by political ones. Similarly, when in 169 the English Parliament passed the '10 per cent' Act, it made it clear that the days when chartered companies could buy from the English Crown the exclusive 'right' to exploit the trade of foreign lands were over.

Even if the increasingly numerous and powerful private traders of Liverpool and Bristol had not challenged the companies' monopolies, two other developments in this century would have proved fatal to those monopolies. One was the ending of the line of the Stuarts, who were chief patrons (and often chief shareholders too) of the chartered companies. The other was the series of wars during this century in which the two chief rivals for the trade of West Africa, Britain and France, found themselves on opposite sides. These wars included the Wars of the English, Spanish and Austrian Successions, the Seven Years' War, the War of American Independence and the Napoleonic Wars. It was quite impossible for any trading company to avoid becoming more and more dependent on its government for protection. It is true that apart from a period of twenty years (1765-85) when Senegambia was a Crown Province, the British Government during this century wanted to confine itself to protecting its subjects' trading interests in West Africa, and did not wish to claim sovereignty there. But in the following century it was to become clear that, for Britain as for France, Portugal, Germany and Spain, it would ultimately become impossible effectively to protect without ruling.

In 1702 the War of the Spanish Succession broke out in Europe. It was to last until 1713. James Fort on the Gambia River, destroyed by the Dutch in 1664 (page 100) and then rebuilt by the English, was soon taken by the French garrison at Goree. As the war went on, the British became stronger both in Europe and in West Africa. The French withdrew from James Fort, and the British reoccupied and strengthened it. When the British launched an attack on the French forts in Goree and Senegal, however, it failed.

But the real enemy of both British and French was their own personnel in West Africa. These officials were servants of the companies trading in the area, the British Royal African Company and the French Senegal Company; but the only interests most of them served were their own. The companies' profits were regularly diverted into their agents' pockets. A chief agent of the British company at James Fort, one Chidley, actually went so far as to counterfeit coins which he substituted for the Company's stock of cash.

In desperation the headquarters of the two rival companies tried in 1705 to agree on marking out a neutral zone in Guinea, cut off from the war in Europe; but this failed because of the disloyalty of the companies' agents. And all the while the British private traders were using to the full the new trading opportunities opened to them at the end of the previous century by the 10 per cent arrangement (page 101). When we learn that, in addition to being disloyal to their employers, the Europeans in James Fort and Goree were frequently drunk and incompetent, we are not surprised that the companies' trade in the area declined steadily at the start of this century. In 1709 James Fort was abandoned, in the same year the Senegal Company was liquidated, and in 1717 Albreda was given up by the French.

And yet British traders were on the eve of their heyday in West Africa, for the treaty of Utrecht of 1713 gave to Britain the 'Asiento' contract for the supply of slaves to America and the West Indies. It was private traders who were to benefit most from these ill-gotten profits. The Royal African Company continued the struggle, however, against its numerous enemies, external and internal. In 1714 it fought off an attempt by the Portuguese to re-establish themselves in the Gambia. Three years later it rebuilt and strengthened James Fort, only to have it stripped by pirates in 1719.

The Company's chief agent at James Fort did not even trouble to report this to his principals in London, and it was from their chief agent in Sierra Leone that news of the disaster reached them. In 1720-1 that agent, Thomas Whitney, sailed to the Gambia with an armed expedition of 170 to try to re-establish the Company's interests there. Illness and pirate attacks took a heavy toll of the members of this expedition, however; and by June 1721 only seventy of them were still alive. Although they succeeded in taking the French forts at Albreda and Bintang (1724) the Company soon found that they had to face fresh trials: they had to fight off a French attack on James Fort in 1724; and in that same year the French recaptured the factories at Bintang and Albreda and seized a British ship. The following year the British company lost another eleven of their men when a magazine of gunpowder blew up on James Fort.

The 1720s in fact saw a fresh burst of activity by the French in the Gambia and Senegal area. In 1721 they expelled the Dutch from Arguin, to which they said that the Treaty of Nimuegen gave them a right; and when the Dutch allied with the Moors of the area and recaptured it the following year, the French gave them only two years to exploit the rich gum trade there before once more expelling them (1724). The French determination to do this had been redoubled by the knowledge that the Dutch were in league with the British in this gum trade.

For a brief period in the 1730s and early 1740s the fortunes of the Royal African Company in the Gambia looked like improving, thanks to the help of the British Government. The British Navy was meeting with increasing success in its attempts to drive pirates from the Guinea coast. From 1730 to 1747 the British Parliament, persuaded that the 10 per cent duty imposed in 1698 was inadequate for the purpose, gave a grant to the Company for the maintenance of its forts. But once again the dishonesty and greed which are only to be expected of slave traders asserted themselves, and public funds joined company profits in the factors' pockets. Above all, a thirty years' breathing space in the wars between Britain and France ended in 1743, and in spite of renewed attempts to agree that West Africa should be regarded as a peaceful neutral area of trade, the attacks of each side on the ships and forts of the other were resumed.

The Treaty of Aix-la-Chapelle (1748) did not settle any disputes in West Africa; and the Royal African Company could not see much of a future for itself. It was dissolved; and in 1750 a new type of company was formed under the name, 'The Company of Merchants Trading to Africa'. Whereas the Royal African Company had been a joint-stock company, the new one was a 'regulated

116

company. Its members could trade separately. They acted as a body only in financing the cost of maintaining the forts, a cost shared also by the British Parliament.

This arrangement seems to have worked quite well for the first fifteen years. French attacks on James Fort from Albreda were resisted, and during the Seven Years' War (1756-63) the British actually captured the French forts in Senegal and Goree, and set fire to Albreda (1758). The Treaty of Paris (1763) returned Albreda and Goree to France, gave Senegal (St Louis) to Britain, and again failed to make a settlement in the Gambia. The French in Guinea were however much less exhausted by the prolonged warfare than the British, partly because their lines of communication were so much shorter. The Peace of Paris (1763) was recognized as being merely the start of another breathing space, and renewed war was sure to come sooner or later, if only to determine the rights of the rivals along the coast south of Senegal. Disheartened, the Company of Merchants invited the British Crown to administer its forts in Senegal and the Gambia. Reluctantly, the British Government agreed, only because it would be cheaper to do so than to continue to subsidize factories managed by incompetent and dishonest drunkards whom the Navy had to be sent to defend whenever an emergency arose.

And so from 1765 to 1785 the Crown Province of Senegambia was ruled by a Governor and Council at St. Louis, who had under him a Lieutenant-Governor on James Island, which served at first mainly as a penal colony.[1] At first, then, Senegal was regarded as much more important than the Gambia. Practically all the troops were at the former post, and O'Hara, the first Governor to be appointed by the Crown, visited the Gambia only twice during his term of office (1765—76). The Lieutenant-Governor in the Gambia was left to do more or less as he wished at first. But renewed warfare in 1778 between Britain and France soon showed the weakness of such an arrangement, when the latter went to the help of the American Colonies in their struggle for independence: in the first year the French captured the Senegal fort, and in the second finally destroyed James Fort.

The Peace of Versailles (1783) found the French strongly entrenched in Senegal, and the British represented in the Gambia by numerous traders, but by no soldiers. The treaty therefore confirmed that Senegal was a French 'possession', and Gambia a British one. The gum trade at Portendic was, however, reserved to the British, and at Albreda and Barra to the French. With nothing but trading interests left to the British by what seemed to be, at last, a final settlement in the area, the British Government handed back to the Committee of the Company of Merchants the administration of the forts in the Gambia.

---

[1] i.e. a colony to which convicts were sent

The truth was that the British Government was now becoming interested in exploration as an opening for trade. It calculated, accurately, that the best way of promoting coastal trade was to plant the flag as far up in the hinterland as possible. In the year of the Peace of Versailles the Society for Promoting the Discovery of the Interior Regions of Africa (often known as the African Association) was founded, with the blessing of the British Government. Under this society's auspices Houghton reached Bambuk through the Gambia (1790) but failed to reach Timbuktu; he was killed probably at Jara. Mungo Park reached the Niger, setting out from the Gambia in 1796.

In 1805 he made a second expedition, this time sailing down the Niger, probably as far as Bussa, where, it is said, he met his death.

It is quite clear that the purpose of these explorations was primarily commercial, and only secondarily scientific. The Society tried to persuade the British Government to send a consul-general to Senegambia 'to exploit the now-proved commercial potential' there. But the Napoleonic Wars (1793-1815) were by now taxing all Britain's resources. From their base in Goree the French sallied out to sack the new British settlement at Freetown (1794), and it was six years before the British were able to collect enough strength on this coast to attack Goree successfully, and at the same time force the French temporarily to abandon Albreda. In the meanwhile, however, another trading rival of the British left the scene when, in 1795, the Dutch East India Company was liquidated. The British might now be the biggest traders on the Upper Gambia and the leading explorers of its hinterland; but the French were still very powerful on the coast, in and above Sierra Leone.

b. SIERRA LEONE

The Royal African Company's interests in Sierra Leone were centred round three factories, as this century opened - at Bunce Island (also spelled 'Bence' and 'Bance'), at Sherbro, and at York Island. These interests were exposed to the same dangers as those in the Gambia - the unprincipled character of the Company's servants, the attacks of pirates, the now legalized competition of the interlopers, and the frequent wars with France.

In 1704, for example, there was an English traitor, thief and murderer called John Leadstone operating on the Sierra Leone River. He had once been one of the Company's servants at Bunce, but had deserted with 1,100 bars of iron - the currency of those days. As the War of the Spanish Succession was then being fought, Leadstone seized the opportunity in that year to help the French to take and pillage the English fort at Bunce, which you will recall had last suffered such a disaster in 1695 (page 106). The following year the same fate befell Sherbro.

The Company decided to rebuild Sherbro at once, and had just completed this in 1709 when fire broke out at York (1710) and destroyed two of the Company's ships and part of the fort.

The Company decided not to repair Bunce and York for the time being. In the meanwhile Leadstone was enjoying himself. We hear of him in 1715 as a pirate off Tasso Island, and his character contrasts significantly with that of the African, Signor Joseph, first missionary on this coast to his own people, who returned that year from his studies in Portugal. Whilst Leadstone was building a nest of pirates at White Man's Bay, Joseph was seeking converts near the present Granville Town, then at Kissy and finally on the Banana Islands. The fact that all along this coast there were many little settlements of Portuguese living permanently there with their African wives, made easier, for different reasons, the activities of both men.

In 1719 and 1720 pirates attacked again the now very vulnerable fort at Bunce, and easily drove away its cowed defenders and took what they wanted. The Company appealed to the British Government for help in dealing with the pirates. As this was during a thirty years' break in warfare between Britain and France (1713-43) (page 116), the British Navy was less fully occupied than at most times during this century; and some at least of the pirates were caught, tried and put to death. Slowly, the Company rebuilt its strength on the Sierra Leone River - in 1721 it had forty-seven servants there.

But a new threat now arose. So far the Temne on the banks of the river had been quite friendly towards the foreign traders, and the forts on this river, like those on the Gold Coast, were designed to protect their occupants from other Europeans. Now, however (1726), the Temne allied with some of the Portuguese settlers persuaded the Temne king to declare that and succeeded in frightening him away. The leader of these Portuguese settlers persuaded the Temne king to declare that trade on the river was free to all except the Company - a ban from which, if it could be enforced, the settlers stood to gain considerably, since they lived by trading on their own account.

The Company abandoned York in 1726, because here too the local inhabitants - Sherbro - were becoming hostile to it. Two years later, after Bunce had again been attacked by Temne and settlers, it too was abandoned, and only York was retained by the Company. Both Temne and Sherbro have been blamed for expelling a company which was paying them rent for the land on which the factories stood; but their action only proves, as did the similar attacks on Elmina and Kommenda (page 109), that the people who owned this land strongly objected to its apparently permanent occupation by foreigners, although they were willing enough to trade.

It was about this time too that the great Muslim Holy War or Jihad started in Futa Jallon, just north of modern Sierra Leone. Here, in a mountainous district, the Muslim Fula whom we met earlier (page 56) set out to convert their pagan

119

Map 11 Sierra Leone

neighbours. Led first by Karamoko Alfa, and then by Ibrahima Sun, they tried, at the point of the sword, to force the Susu and the non-Muslim Fula to accept Islam. Many Susu left and moved south to settle in Limba and Temne country; the Yalunka, who also had lived in Futa Jallon, similarly left, later settling in Falaba.

Bunce Island was taken over by a firm of three partners in London who, failing to learn from the Royal African Company's mistakes, tried to make

The Eighteenth Century – Slaves and Factories

treaties' with the Temne king, and rebuilt the fort. Most of the 3,000 slaves being sold at this time from the Sierra Leone River each year were, however, passing through the hands of private traders, such as the one who employed the hymn-writing John Newton in the Plantain Islands in 1745. Soon after this, as we have seen, the Royal African Company gave place to the regulated Company of Merchants (page 116), and during the disturbed conditions of the Seven Years' War and the War of American Independence the ships of many nations were to be seen in the Sierra Leone River.

The latter war affected Sierra Leone in many ways. One of these was to increase the demand in America for slaves to replace those who had seized the opportunity offered them by the war to recover their freedom by running away from their masters and joining the British Army or Navy. So more and more traders came to the Sierra Leone River looking for slaves. The London company leased the Bunce fort[1] to a private slave trader who rebuilt it (1786) and then died (1790). A Liverpool firm set up a trading post on the south bank, but gave it up when its agent was murdered (1770). The French Government 'rented' land in 1784 from the Temne king, Forbana, on an island in the estuary for 100 iron bars a year plus £1,200 payable over the first two years; but the island was too small and unhealthy, and the trading post they set up was closed in 1793. In 1785 the Liverpool firm tried again to establish a factory on the same spot as before, but this time cautiously kept its chief agent on the Isles de Los near Conakry.[2] Gambia Island, near Bunce, was by now a nest of French interlopers, who remained there until 1793.

Meanwhile two important inland peoples had been moving slowly towards the coast. The Vai, the only West African people who are known to have invented their own script, had moved during this century down to the Gallinas area near Cape Mount.[3] It is possible that they were the remnants of the powerful Mani, and certain that they are related to the modern Kono in the eastern province of Sierra Leone. The Mende, today Sierra Leone's largest people, had by the end of this century also moved into Sierra Leone from the east, and were settling in what is today its southern province, bringing with them a strong military tradition of stockaded towns and spartan secret societies.

It was on to this colourful scene that there sailed on May 9, 1787, the 411 persons who represent in Sierra Leone's history the second main effect of the War of American Independence. These were the original settlers of Freetown, freed negro slaves and their white wives, all alike collected from the streets of London. During the next eighty years they were to be followed by three more groups of immigrants. First there were 1,190 freed slaves who had been

---

[1] See map p. 85
[2] See map p. 85
[3] See map p. 85

121

unhappily settled by the British in Nova Scotia after the War of American Independence, and were resettled in the new colony of Freetown in 1792. Then there were 500 Maroons, freed slaves, mostly of Asante origin, from Jamaica, who, having similarly failed to settle down in Novia Scotia, were sent to Freetown in 1800. Finally there were the 40,000 'liberated Africans' who had not crossed the Atlantic at all, but were removed from the slave ships of many nations by British warships patrolling off the West African coast between 1807 (when Britain declared the slave trade illegal for its subjects) and about 1864, when the transatlantic slave trade finally stopped.

Most historians have claimed that both the founding of Freetown in 1787 and Britain's action in making the slave trade unlawful (it was not effectively abolished until about 1864) were the achievements of a movement inspired by humanitarianism and philanthropy (that is, love of one's fellow humans), aroused in some way by a group of Christians in Britain. This was no doubt true of the earlier movement, led by Granville Sharp, which secured a ruling in 1772 by Lord Chief Justice Mansfield that English law did not recognize slavery. But the later movement, led by Thomas Clarkson, Granville Sharp, Henry Thornton, Zachary Macaulay and William Wilberforce (their spokesman in the British Parliament), also had definite commercial motives. At first (1785-90) it was inspired by a concern to preserve the value of property in some of the districts of London. Streets in these districts had become filled with unemployed negro ex-slaves, who had been freed either by Mansfield's judgment or by running away from their masters during the War of American Independence and fighting on the British side. The Committee for the Black Poor, formed by the 'philanthropists' to resettle the freed slaves, was doing, in a different way, what the 1962 Commonwealth Immigration Act seeks to do.

This is why what the Committee regarded as yet another form of unsightly human litter on London's streets - poverty- ridden white women - were also swept up and placed on the Freetown-bound ships, although it would have been easy to provide the settlers with much better wives from amongst other ex-slaves. This is also why very little thought was given by the Committee as to where the settlers should go, when they should arrive and how they should be equipped. Freetown, picturesque as it is, has far less land suitable for farming than the Accra plains, for example; it has also, between May and September, a fearsome rainy season. Yet to this spot they were sent in May, equipped with tents and hoes, to settle on the site of the modern State House, and to die there like flies, before being finally wiped out by the Temne king, Jimmy, in 1789, in revenge for the burning of his town by a British warship. It is also why, although this shortlived settlement (known as the 'Province of Freedom') was completely self-governing, the British Government was willing to pay the cost of transporting and equipping the settlers, instead of leaving the whole expense to the Committee.

In 1790 it occurred to Clarkson and his friends that certain 'treaties' thumbprinted by the Temne kings, Tom and Naimbana, of Sierra Leone in 1787 and 1788 'giving up' land to the now collapsed 'Province of Freedom' for a total payment of £144, could be turned to good commercial use. A trading company was formed the following year with, significantly, a banker (Henry Thornton), *not* a 'philanthropist', as chairman; and it was this company, the Sierra Leone Company, which settled both the Nova Scotians (1792) and the Maroons (1800) on the site of the old Province of Freedom, and on the land immediately to the east of it as far as modern Kissy. But this new settlement was not self-governing. The Directors of the Company appointed the Governor, the first holder of the post (1792) being Thomas Clarkson's brother John, who had captained the naval expedition which transported the Nova Scotians to Freetown. The new settlers, under the Governor, were expected to do the same as the Portuguese settlements we have already noted and the French interlopers (page 101) had been doing so successfully - namely, trade with the Temne; but with two big differences. The freed slaves were to deal, on the European side, only with the Sierra Leone Company; and they were forbidden to deal in slaves. They were encouraged to grow cotton and coffee for sale to the Company.

The settlers from Nova Scotia, being so much more numerous and better equipped than those from London, fared much better. But the warfare between France and Britain was resumed in 1793 and extensive looting of the Company's property in a French attack in 1794 prevented the Company from showing a profit. Then, just before the Maroons arrived in 1800, the leaders of the Nova Scotians rebelled against Governor Ludlam, who was saved only by the arrival of the troops escorting the Maroons. The following year a war began between the colony and the Temne which lasted for six years. As a result the colonists, who had the best of the fighting, occupied all the peninsula west of the original settlement (i.e. between Tower Hill and Cape Aberdeen). But the purpose for which the Sierra Leone Company had been founded was being defeated, as trade was impossible. The Company had also hoped that the new colony would be a torch-bearer of European education and religion, as well as a base for European exploration of the hinterland. The hostility of the Temne had crushed all these hopes. The Company, which had steadily made a loss, now looked for someone to take over responsibility for a colony whose very survival was a vast tribute to the negro's resilience and resourcefulness in most unfavourable circumstances.

In the meantime Wilberforce had persuaded the British Parliament, and his friends had persuaded many outside Parliament, that the British economy would now be better served by trading with negroes than by trading in them. The Industrial Revolution had made this a convincing argument, and it was used just as often as saying that the slave trade was cruel. So Britain followed in 1807 the lead given by Denmark two years earlier, and passed an Act declaring the slave trade illegal. The U.S.A. followed in 1808, Sweden in 1813 and Holland in 1814.

We must remember, though, that the slave trade was abolished largely because it had now become more profitable to seek in West Africa raw materials and markets, rather than slaves.

But Britain went further. The war between the Freetown settlers and the Temne had just ended; if the British Government took the colony off the bankrupt company's hands Britain would remain in a stronger position than any other European country, both in putting to the test the abolitionists' arguments about trade and in continuing the exploration of the interior which was essential to success in that trade.

So on January 1, 1808, in Freetown, as had happened in 1765 at St Louis (page 117), a Crown Colony was created in West Africa, and the Union Jack was run up. Sovereignty, 'given away' unsuspectingly to the first settlers by Kings Tom and Naimbana (1787-8), recovered temporarily by King Jimmy (1789) and seized again by the Sierra Leone Company (1791), was now (1808) handed to the British Crown, which was not to return it to the people of Sierra Leone until April 27, 1961.

C. THE GOLD COAST

The eighteenth century saw the continuation in the Gold Coast of the struggle for trade between British, French and Dutch traders, some of them in the service of companies, others trading on their own account. The new trend here during this century was the steady growth in unity and strength of the Asante nation, and the beginning of a four-sided hostility between that nation, the Fante, the British and the Dutch.

At the beginning of the century the Asante were not in direct contact with the Europeans. They sent their trading commodities to the coast either through middlemen such as the Begho people (page 110) in the case of gold, or, in the case of slaves, to a large slave market at Manso, thirty miles from the coast. Here Fante middlemen were waiting to buy the slaves and take them to smaller collecting points on the coast, from which the Europeans bought them.

But the Asante were impatient at having to deal with middle men; and as their strength grew they saw less and less reason why this should continue. They tried to outflank the Fante, and we find them appearing more and more frequently in western forts such as Dixcove, Sekondi, Shama, Kommenda, Elmina and Cape Coast, and in eastern forts such as Accra and Prampram. The British, who also stood to gain by avoiding using middlemen, helped and encouraged the Asante in this.

Then between 1738 and 1745 the Asante found their way to the coast blocked by a group of peoples who, whilst not middlemen, were afraid that the growing night of Asante might turn against them if allowed to come too near their borders. In the west Wassaw, Denkyera and Twifo were the leaders of this group, and in the east Akim and Akwamu. The eastern barrier the Asante found particularly difficult to pass, as those states lay physically between Asante and Fante. The Wassaw, on the other hand, had to leave their own territory to prevent the Asante reaching the coast. Moreover, relations between Wassaw and Fante were frequently hostile, and the Wassaw found themselves sometimes fighting two powerful enemies at the same time.

In the meantime the Europeans continued to trade with, and occasionally to convert, whom they could. In 1750 the Anglican priest Thomas Thompson settled at Cape Coast, and sent for training in England a lad who was to become the first Negro priest on this coast, Philip Quacoe. Quacoe was to preach Christianity on the Gold Coast from 1766 to 1816.

In 1760 the Asante and Fante formed a somewhat uneasy alliance against their mutual enemy the Wassaw. The latter were saved by the accession to the Asante throne in 1764 of Osei Kojo, a far more ambitious and aggressive ruler than his predecessor Kusi Obodum. Kojo marched against Wassaw, it is true; but he also turned on his predecessors' allies the Fante, and on the Akim. He defeated the latter in the east, but shortage of food forced him to end his campaign unsuccessfully in the west. The Fante quickly formed an alliance with the Wassaw and Twifo to meet any future Asante advance, and Osei Kojo was compelled to confine himself to the eastern route to the coast, through Akim to Accra and Prampram. Skirmishes continued between his forces and the western allies, however, especially between 1765 and 1767, and again in 1772-3, as he tried again to gain direct access to the coastal trade in that area.

The British continued to control most of this trade. In 1757 the French had tried to capture Cape Coast Castle, but had been foiled. Soon after this the British erected a fort in Nzima, at Beyin, and called it 'Apollonia'. Recognizing the Dutch as their most powerful rivals, they attacked their forts whenever they could. Attacks on the Dutch fort at Elmina failed in 1780 and 1781, but in the latter year the British had a round of successes against the Dutch, whose forts at Mori, Apam, Kormantine, Beraku, Kommenda and Crevecœur all fell into British hands. The only Dutch success to offset against this in this year was their capture of the British fort at Sekondi.

Yet it is typical of the waste of effort, men and money by Europeans on this coast at this time that by the end of 1783 all the Dutch losses had been recovered. Sekondi was destroyed by its captors and was never rebuilt. In fact what the Europeans on this coast were doing was to exhaust themselves so thoroughly against one another that they were forced to seek allies amongst the local kings if they were to preserve their interests.

These allies were usually won by bribery. As early as 1708 Sir Dalby Thomas, the Royal African Company's chief agent at Cape Coast Castle, had advised his principals in London not to try to economize on gifts to the Asantehene, with whom he felt it would be worth trying to establish direct trade In 1774 the Committee of the Company of London Merchants received a report from their representative at Cape Coast saying frankly: 'Knowing we have not sufficient power to protect ourselves . . . it is necessary to keep black men of power in our pay.'

Until 1765 the British used their influence over the King of Asante to encourage him to come to the coast to trade with them. After that date, however they sought to prevent the Fante from becoming subject to the Asante; for by now the latter had grown so powerful as to threaten to control, rather than be controlled by, their former British allies. So British policy was to bolster Fante power just enough to check the Asante, but not enough to enable the Fante to develop strength and unity on the scale the Asante had done.

The Dutch in the 1760s similarly shamelessly used local peoples as pawns, in their constant scheming to get the better of the British. The people of Nzima (see map page 61) were bitterly opposed to the Dutch at this time, and the British claimed that they built the fort at Beyin because the Nzima asked for protection against the Dutch. It was the Asante whose friendship was at this time most constantly cultivated by the Dutch as a counterweight to the Fante-British link.

But in 1765, when it looked for a time as though the great Osei Kojo would conquer the Fante, the Europeans were very quick to put aside their rivalries against a threat which might expel them all from the Gold Coast. Dutch and British offered jointly to act as mediators between Asante and Fante to re establish the state of uneasy peace which helped the Europeans to do good business. In this they relied largely on extensive bribery.

The Asante-Fante hostility almost came to a head again in 1792, when the Danish governor of Christiansborg Castle allied with the Asantehene Osei Kwame against the Fante. The Asantehene had for years claimed to be the ground landlord of nearby James Fort, an English 'possession', dating back this claim to the defeat of the Akim by Opoku Ware. The Asante marched on Accra to link up with the soldiers of their Danish ally and then plan a campaign against the British and Fante. Only the sudden death of the Governor of Christiansborg broke up the alliance, his more timid successor persuading the Asante to return home, by means of lavish 'presents'. It was clear however that a full-scale war between Asante and Fante could not be delayed much beyond the end of th century, not even by bribery on the scale British and Dutch practised it on this coast at this time.

d. THE SLAVE COAST

During the eighteenth century, whilst Benin was continuing the decline which Bosman had noted in 1703 (page 111), Oyo was growing in strength. We have seen Alafin Ojigi's crushing defeat of Dahomey's coastal vassal Great Ardra in 1698 (page 112). In 1724 the King of Dahomey determined to make a supreme effort to extend his frontiers southwards to the sea and so gain access through Porto Novo to the lucrative coastal trade. But he could now do this only at the expense of Oyo. It seemed as if it was going to be an uneven battle. Oyo was 300 years old, and growing. Dahomey was 100 years old, and much smaller in every respect. Yet such was the determination of the people of Dahomey that they survived a number of defeats by the Alafin's cavalry; then when the Oyo, with the aid of Porto Novo palm wine, had celebrated a little too well their victories, the Dahomeyans turned on the drunken Oyo soldiers and killed or routed them all (1724).

However, everyone must have known that the Alafin would not let it rest at that. He waited for an opportunity to take a decisive revenge on his daring little neighbour. This came in 1727, when Dahomey, seeking another route to the coast, attacked Oyo's ally Ouidah (page 111). The Alafin hardly waited for Ouidah to ask for help. He looted so many of Dahomey's outlying villages that its king begged for mercy. Oyo agreed for the time being to accept tribute from Dahomey, but ten years later decided to move against Dahomey's capital itself, Abomey. It took another ten years before the stout-hearted fighters of Abomey would finally surrender; but when they did so, in 1747, they had to agree to pay Oyo an annual tribute of eighty slaves, forty guns and 4,000 head-loads of cowrie shells a year with effect from the date of their first defeat, 1727. They continued to pay this heavy tribute until the 1780s.

By then, however, Oyo's strength was being sapped, not by external attack, but by internal political feuds and by the distance between its capital and its coastal vassals. The Alafin's chief minister held the title of Basorun, and was a member of the Oyo Mesi, the Council of State (page 112). Basorun Gaha, who came to power in 1747, constantly plotted against his Alafin, and not until about 1787 did the Alafin, with the help of his Kakanfo or army chief, regain control over his chief minister. But these forty years of divided authority in Oyo were fatal to its hold over its vassals. First Dahomey, and then the Egba, threw off Oyo's rule, King Adahoozu of Dahomey simply ceasing to send to King Abiodun of Oyo the tribute agreed upon in 1747, and the Egba actually defeating an Oyo army. A great empire had begun to disintegrate; but it was not until 1817, when Ilorin broke away with the help of the Fulani, that this became clear to all.

Even Benin at the beginning of this century, though very weak externally, must not be thought of as disorganized internally. Bosman, who had in 1703 noted its 'half-remaining houses' (page 111), also noted that its laws were just, its traders honest, and its people well provided for and hospitable. This was perhaps because the focal point of European slave trade, having done its worst at the western end of the Slave Coast, was moving east to the Niger and Cross River estuaries. Here Ijaw, Efik and Warri peoples usually enslaved not one another but Ibo and Onitsha to the north, and sold them to the Europeans in increasing numbers throughout the century. The annual rate at which Ibo were being sold into slavery by 1800 has been estimated at 18,000. For reasons we do not yet fully understand, their culture did not survive transatlantic transplantation as well as that of the Yoruba from whom most of the slaves had been taken in the seventeenth century. Yet we can still find in Cuba, Trinidad and Haiti traces of Ibo, Ibibio and Efik cultures.

Meanwhile to the north of the Slave Coast, Katsina was, by 1800, the leading military and commercial state, whilst Bornu, particularly in the second half of this century, when the Mai line ruled, was the leader in learning and culture. Kano was suffering a military decline during this century, defeated by Zamfara, a sister Hausa state, in 1700, and under heavy attack by another, Gobir, between 1731 and 1743. Gobir and Zamfara were at this time allies; but in 1764 the former defeated the latter and destroyed its capital Birnin; and the Zamfarawa had to seek the help of powerful Katsina to enable them to rebuild their capital at Anka. Thus by the end of the century we have two strong Hausa states, Katsina and Gobir, who were however weakening each other by constant warfare; and three relatively weak states, Bornu, Zamfara and Kano, with Bornu's scholarly Mai rulers giving that state a deserved reputation as a centre of Hausa culture.

Throughout Hausaland, however, there was spreading by the end of this century a feeling of alarm which was tending to cause the rulers to close their ranks. It was caused by the steadily growing domination of Hausa society by the Fulani Gidda. These were the urban and fanatically Muslim section of the non-negro Fula people whom we met earlier in the Gambia and Futa Jallon (page 75). The alarm started when the Fulani attacked the Jukun of Kororofa (page 113) in the 1790s; for it was known that the attackers were wealthy, influential, intelligent and skilful in arms. Moreover, they had already shown contempt for what they said was the disloyalty to Islam shown by many of the Hausa. All that the Fulani needed in 1800 in order to conquer Hausaland was a leader. At the teacher's desk in the nursery of the palace of Nafata, King of Gobir, a Fulani scholar named Usman dan Fodio coached the king's children, and patiently bided his time.

SUGGESTED QUESTIONS

CHAPTER 1
(a) How do historians learn how illiterate people lived many centuries ago?
(b) How did climate affect the history of West Africa?
(c) Describe the life of Sangoan man.
(d) Do the tools and clay utensils still in use in villages in your country resemble in any way those you see in museums? Explain both the differences and the similarities.
(e) Make a time chart which shows the periods at which Western Europeans, West Africans, and Egyptians, respectively, passed through their Neolithic Age.

CHAPTER 2
(a) List the new nations which have come into existence in West Africa since the Second World War.
(b) What reasons have you found for the fact that great civilizations seem so often to have developed in river valleys?
(c) Why did the ancient Persians hold the 'Ethiopians' in such respect? Do you think it was fear of a people they did not really know, admiration for their supposed wealth, or some sounder reason?
(d) What do you think led classical writers about West Africa to make so many mistakes about the source and the direction of the Niger?
(e) How did geography prevent West Africans and Europeans from close contact with and knowledge of each other for so many centuries?

CHAPTER 3
(a) Describe the religious and social life of ancient Ghana.
(b) In what lay that country's wealth?
(c) Which mineral was in the long run of greater importance in the history of the Empire of Ghana — gold or iron? Why?
(d) Relate how this Empire was governed at the height of its power.
(e) Why did the Empire of Ghana fall?

CHAPTER 4
(a) Would you agree that the Empire of Mali was at one time 'one of the greatest states in the world'?
(b) Describe the life and death of Emperor Sundiata of Mali.
(c) Imagine that you have travelled to Mali with Ibn Batuta. Describe what impressed you most.

(d) Why do you think such a wealthy and powerful Empire as Mali lasted so short a time?

(e) List the similarities you have noticed between the social customs in ancient Mali and those in your own country.

CHAPTER 5

(a) Trace on an outline map the most important trade routes from North to West Africa before the coming of the Europeans.

(b) Why did the Songhai choose the site of modern Gao as their capital?

(c) How did Islam reach West Africa, and why did it spread so rapidly?

(d) Who do you think was the greatest of the Songhai kings, and why?

(e) List the most important towns in this Empire, and describe the contribution of each to the country's wealth.

CHAPTER 6

(a) How did the state of Bornu-Kanem come into existence?

(b) How was it governed?

(c) Name the fourteen Hausa states, and explain their importance in West African history.

(d) Why do you think these states remained so small and disunited?

(e) How did the long Sefuwa line of Bornu kings come to an end?

CHAPTER 7

(a) Describe some of the traditions about the origins of the Akan and of Kumasi.

(b) What is the importance of Anoyke in Akan history?

(c) What was the cause of the battle of Feyase, and what its result?

(d) How did Opoku Ware enlarge Asante?

(e) What do you think would have halted the spread of Asante power, if European gunpowder and slave trading had not done so? Would it have rivalled that of ancient Ghana?

CHAPTER 8

(a) Describe how Ife and Oyo are recorded as having been founded, and describe the relations between the two states.

(b) Describe the role of the Fulani in West African history before the coming of the Europeans.

(c) Describe the 'lost wax' method of bronze casting, and relate how it reached the Edos of Benin.

(d) Why was Benin so dependent on Ife?

(e) What effect did the European slave trade have on the policy of the rulers of Oyo and Benin, and on the fortunes of their states?

CHAPTER 9

a) Describe Henry the Navigator's contribution to Europe's knowledge of West Africa.

b) What two serious mistakes did the Portuguese in W.A. make in this century?

c) Describe briefly some of the peoples found in W.A. by Europeans in the fifteenth and sixteenth centuries.

d) Describe how and where the first European forts on the Gold Coast came to be built.

e) What do you know of the trade between São Tome, Gwato, Elmina and Lisbon?

f) What does Pacheco Pereira tell us about Benin?

CHAPTER 10

a) Describe the arrival of the first Christian missionaries in W.A.

b) What do you know about the Mani of Sierra Leone?

c) What does Alvares d'Almada tell us about Sierra Leone in 1594?

d) What effects did the conquest of Portugal by Spain in 1580 have on W.A.?

e) Which nations were in turn most successful in exploiting the trade of W.A. in the sixteenth century, and why?

f) Why was the 'Company of Merchant Adventurers for Guinea' formed?

g) Give some account of the transatlantic slave trade, and of the trade in domestic slaves sent from W.A. to Europe.

h) Describe the trade between W.A. and Europe in commodities other than slaves during this century.

CHAPTER 11

a) How did the wars between England and Holland in this century affect the history of W.A.?

b) Mention some of the European companies trading in W.A. in this century, and some of the difficulties they experienced.

c) Describe some of the peoples who lived along what is now the Nigerian coast during this century.

d) What cultural reminders of the slave trade still survive in the New World?

e) 'The Europeans in W.A. in the seventeenth century were more a threat to morale than to sovereignty.' Say whether, and why, you agree or disagree.

f) Trace the history of the rivalry between the English companies and the interlopers which ended in 1698.

g) What was the important change in the direction of trade through Ashanti during this century, and why did it occur?

h) What do you know about the Mani and Temne?

CHAPTER 12

(a) Give illustrations of the disloyalty of European company officials to their employers during this century.

(b) How did the series of wars in Europe during this century affect trading fortunes in W.A.?

(c) Why did Senegambia become a Province of the British Crown in 1765, and lose that status in 1785?

(d) What do you know about the African Association?

(e) Describe the activities of John Leadstone in Sierra Leone.

(f) How did relations between British, Dutch, Fante and Asante change during this century?

(g) What were the causes of the persistent hostility between the Asante and their southern neighbours during this century?

(h) Describe and account for some of Oyo's successes, and some of its failures against other states during this century.

(i) Which were, at the end of this century, the leading states in the north of what is today Nigeria?

TIME CHART

Some related events are shown in italics. Each class is advised to add others

DATE	SENEGAMBIA	SIERRA LEONE	GHANA	NIGERIA
1419			*[Henry the Navigator founded naval academy at Sagres*	
1434	Gil Eannes rounded Cape Bojador			
1441	Portuguese passed Cape Blanco. Gold and slaves taken			
1442	to Portugal (from Rio De Oro)			
1443	Portuguese reached Arguin			
1445	First treaty signed, after Nuno Tristao rounded Cape Verde	Alvaro Fernandes first sighted S.L. coast		
1448	Tristao passed R. Gambia, killed on Rio Grande			
1455	Henry the Navigator sent two expeditions to the Gambia			
1456	Another Portuguese expedition to the Gambia			

West Africa in History

DATE	SENEGAMBIA	SIERRA LEONE	GHANA	NIGERIA
1458	Henry's 3rd expedition to the Gambia			
1460		Portuguese reached Sierra Leone		
			[Henry the Navigator died	
1461		Portuguese passed Liberian coast		
			[Afonso V continued Henry's work	
1462		Pedro da Sintra mapped S.L. coast		
1466	Cape Verde Islanders given monopoly of trade north of Sierra Leone			
1469		Fernão Gomes given monopoly of trade south of S.L.		
1471			Joao de Santarem and Pedro de Esobar landed on Gold Coast	
1472			Portuguese set up factory at Shama	
1475	Portuguese began abducting slaves			

Time Chart

DATE	SENEGAMBIA	SIERRA LEONE	GHANA	NIGERIA
1480			[*Spain and Portugal signed agreement about Guinea trade*	
1481		John Tintan and William Fabian entered S.L. river mouth	Portuguese began construction of Elmina castle [*John II succeeded Afonso V in Portugal*	
1482	John II of Portugal completed Arguin castle	Portuguese began to build fort on Tombo Island	[*Portugal forced England to abandon proposed Guinea expedition*	
1483	French reached Cape Verde	Portuguese set up factory at Port Loko		Fernão do Po visited Benin
1484	Portuguese reached the Congo			
1485				Diego Cam visited Benin. São Tomé traded direct with Benin
1486				Portuguese priests arrived in Benin. Gwato fort closed temporarily
1487	Portuguese took Joloff King Bemoi to Portugal to be baptized			
			[*Bartholomew Dias reached the Cape of Good Hope*	
1491	Portuguese expedition to Kantora			

135

West Africa in History

DATE	SENEGAMBIA	SIERRA LEONE	GHANA	NIGERIA
1492			French priva-teers captured Portuguese ship leaving Elmina	
1494			[*Treaty of Tordesillas*	
1495		Portuguese com-pleted Tombo Fort		
1497			[*Vasco da Gama reached India*	
1500	French, Spanish and English in-terlopers chal-lenging Portu-guese monopoly		Two Portuguese convoys sailing between Lisbon and Elmina annually [*Fernão de Mello became Captain of São Tomé*	
1501	Portuguese be-gan small settle-ments in Sene-gambia			
1502			[*Spaniard Nicolas de Ovando carried first slaves across the Atlantic*	
1503			French captured 300 Portuguese ships between 1500 and 1503. Portuguese built Axim Fort	
1507			Little Portuguese trade, owing to interlopers	Pereira described Benin in *Esmer-aldo de situ orbis*
1510			[*First West African slaves taken to gold mines in Hispaniola*	

Time Chart

DATE	SENEGAMBIA	SIERRA LEONE	GHANA	NIGERIA
1513		Portuguese began small settlements in S.L.		
1520				Gwato fort finally abandoned by Portuguese
1522			[*Fernão de Mello, Captain of São Tomé, died*	
1526			Portuguese built fort at Shama	
1527			Portuguese fort on Gold Coast commanded by Pereira at Elmina	
1540				Oba of Benin sent envoy to Portugal
1550			English succeeded French as most active interlopers	
1551			French most active of interlopers	
1553			Thomas Windham's ships sailed to Elmina from Portsmouth	Windham's ships reached Benin
1554			Lok's ships reached Shama	

West Africa in History

DATE	SENEGAMBIA	SIERRA LEONE	GHANA	NIGERIA
1555			Towerson's ships traded on the Gold Coast, allying with French	
1556			Towerson's 2nd expedition. Watch-tower built at Elmina	
1558			Towerson's 3rd expedition *[Elizabeth I's accession to the English throne*	
1561		Mani began to move north-westwards from Cape Mount	*[Co. of Merchant Adventurers for Guinea formed in England*	
1570			Comani and Fetu people attacked Elmina	
1576			Portuguese built fort at Accra	
1580			*[Philip II of Spain conquered Portugal*	
1588	'Sale' of Gambia trade to English merchants approved by Elizabeth I			
1594		Alvares d'Almada described S.L.		
1595			First Dutch voyages to the Gold Coast	

Time Chart

DATE	SENEGAMBIA	SIERRA LEONE	GHANA	NIGERIA
1598	Elizabeth I transferred claim to Gambia trade to Nottingham and Stanhope		Dutch built factories at Butri, Kormantine, Mori and Kommenda	
1599		Mani defeated by Fulam cavalry		
1600			Kobia Amanfi became Asantehene about now	
1605		Philip III of Spain sent Jesuit Balthazar Barreira to Tombo site at Kroo Bay acquired for Spanish fort		
1606		Barreira founded church in S.L.		
1607		William Keeling's voyage to S.L.		
1609		Barreira left S.L.		
1610		Mani Emperor Touray died	[During the early years of this century Spain and Portugal were becoming less active commercially, and England, France and Holland more active. Denmark and Germany were beginning to take an interest in West African trade	

West Africa in History

DATE	SENEGAMBIA	SIERRA LEONE	GHANA	NIGERIA
1612	French tried to erect fort on Gambia River			
1617			[*Dutch West India Co. set up. English Co. of Adventurers of London Trading to Guinea and Benin set up*	
1620	Explorer Jobson refused to take slaves. Fula had reached Senegambia			
1621	Dutch West India Co. set up factory on Goree Island			
1622			[*Dutch had 40 ships in W.A. trade*	
1623			Portuguese extended their activities from Elmina to Aowin	
1624			People of Aowin and Elmina attacked Portuguese Elmina	
1625			Dutch at Mori also attacked Portuguese	Kingdom of Dahomey founded about now
1627	Dutch West India Co. sent ships to Gambia between now and 1636			
1629			[*English Co. of Adventurers of London Trading to Guinea and Benin failed*	

Time Chart

DATE	SENEGAMBIA	SIERRA LEONE	GHANA	NIGERIA
1630			Oti Akenten succeeded Kobia Amanfi as Asantehene about now *[English Co. of Merchants Trading to Guinea set up*	
1633	French Senegal Co. given monopoly of Senegal and Gambia trade for 30 years			
1636			Elmina workings collapsed. Elmina people attacked Portuguese	
1637			Portuguese fled to Axim after Dutch attack *[Dutch seized Brazil, and supplied it with W. African slaves*	
1638	Dutch W. I. Company captured Portuguese fort at Arguin			
1640		Dutch base at Gallinas abandoned	*[Portugal and Spain separated*	
1642		Capuchin priest Seraphim building churches at Port Loko and Tombo	Dutch captured Portuguese Axim. Portuguese left western Gold Coast	

West Africa in History

DATE	SENEGAMBIA	SIERRA LEONE	GHANA	NIGERIA
1644				Olu of Warri said to be descended from Portuguese
1647	12 Capuchin monks arrived			
1650		Portuguese now on Scarcies only	Portuguese now at Christiansborg only	
1651		English Co. of Merchants started building factories in Sherbro	Begho people began to trade southwards instead of northwards [*English Co. of London Merchants formed*	
1652	English Co. of London Merchants sent unsuccessful expedition to Gambia		Swedes completed chain of forts at Takoradi, Cape Coast, Osu	
1653				Jukun of Kororofa attacked Kano
1657		Company of London Merchants handed Sherbro factories to East India Co.	Company of London Merchants handed G.C. forts to East India Co.	
1658			Danes captured all Swedish forts	

142

Time Chart

DATE	SENEGAMBIA	SIERRA LEONE	GHANA	NIGERIA
1660			Obiri Yeboa succeeded Oti Akenten as Asantehene about now	
1661		Royal Adventurers' Captain Holmes trading with S.L.	Royal Adventurers took over Gold Coast forts [*Royal Adventurers of England Trading into Africa formed*	
1662		Holmes built Tasso Fort	Cape Coast and Egya taken by Dutch from English	
1663	English 'Adventurers' took James and Charles Islands	Royal Adventurers built Bunce Fort and · took over Sherbro factories		
1664	Dutch Admiral de Ruyter destroyed James Fort	Dutch Admiral de Ruyter destroyed Tasso Fort	English Captain Holmes re-covered forts from Dutch, seized others [*French West India Companies set up during the next 10 years*	
1665	English rebuilt James Fort		Dutch Admiral de Ruyter re-gained forts	
1667	Revolt of slaves on James Island			
1668			[*English Co. of Gambia Adventurers set up*	
1670		Capuchin mission in Tombo and Port Loko closed	Adansi invaded Tafo	

143

West Africa in History

DATE	SENEGAMBIA	SIERRA LEONE	GHANA	NIGERIA
1671				Jukun of Koro-rofa attacked Kano and Katsina
1672	Royal African Co. bought Royal Adventurers' forts in G.C., S.L. and the Gambia for £34,000 [*Royal African Co. succeeded Royal Adventurers of England*]			
1673			Danes sold Cape Coast Fort to English [*Gambia Adventurers dissolved*]	
1674			Danes abandoned Takoradi Fort to English [*French W.I. Co. dissolved. French Senegal Co. revived*]	
1675			Royal African Co. built James Fort and others, rebuilt still more [*French Senegal Co. seized Goree from Dutch*]	
1678	French seized Arguin Fort from Dutch		[*Dutch W.I. Co.'s interest in W.A. ended*]	
1679			Portuguese acquired Christiansborg [*French now succeeded Dutch as England's chief rivals in W.A.*]	
1680				Jukun of Koro-rofa attacked Bornu successfully

Time Chart

DATE	SENEGAMBIA	SIERRA LEONE	GHANA	NIGERIA
1681	French renting site of Albreda factory from local king		Elmina people attacked Dutch Conraadsborg fort	
1682			Portuguese finally left the Gold Coast	Olu of Warri said to be married to a Portuguese
1683		French pirate Jean Hamlin captured 17 English and Dutch ships in S.L.		
1685		Warehouse in Bunce destroyed by fire		
1686	French factory at Albreda burnt down and rebuilt. Another built at Geregia			
1687		Bunce factor John Case robbed of ivory by Dutch pirate		
1688		Sherbro factory abandoned to strengthen York. Bunce attacked by French		
1689	French factories at Albreda and Geregia destroyed by English			

West Africa in History

DATE	SENEGAMBIA	SIERRA LEONE	GHANA	NIGERIA
1690			[English merchant James Barbot visited West Africa	
1692	French forts at Senegal and Goree in English hands, until 1693			
1694			Dutch and Elmina fought Fante, Kommenda and Asebu	
1695	English fort on James Island destroyed by French	Bunce again attacked by French, and sacked		
1697		Temne increasing in strength	Osei Tutu succeeded Obiri Yeboa as Asantehene about now	
1698	English rebuilt fort on James Island			Alafin Ojigi of Oyo defeated Dahomey's vassal Great Ardra
			[Peace of Ryswick Act at Westminster opened trade in W.A.	
1700				Kano defeated by Zamfara
1702	French garrison of Goree took James Fort			
1703				Bosman described Benin

Time Chart

DATE	SENEGAMBIA	SIERRA LEONE	GHANA	NIGERIA
1704	French withdrew from James Fort	Pirate John Leadstone helped French to sack Bunce Fort		
1705		Sherbro Fort sacked by French		
1707	British re-occupied James Fort			
1708	British failed to take French forts in Goree and Senegal		Sir Dalby Thomas, Chief Agent at Cape Coast, advocated bribing of Asantehene	
1709	James Fort abandoned by British	Rebuilding of Sherbro completed		
			[*Senegal Company liquidated*	
1710		A fire at York destroyed part of the fort and two ships		
1712			Osei succeeded Osei Tutu as Asantehene about now	
1713			[*Treaty of Utrecht, and 'Asiento'*	
1714	Portuguese tried but failed to re-establish themselves on Gambia			

West Africa in History

DATE	SENEGAMBIA	SIERRA LEONE	GHANA	NIGERIA
1715		Pirate Leadstone operating off Tasso Island		
1716		Signor Joseph, first African missionary, began work		
1717	James Fort strengthened by Royal African Co. Albreda given up to French		End of Osei's reign as Asantehene	
1719	Pirates stripped James Fort	Pirates pillaged Bunce		
1720	Royal African Co.'s S.L. Agent Thomas Whitney took armed expedition to Gambia	Another pillaging of Bunce by pirates	Opoku Ware became Asantehene	
1721	French expelled Dutch from Arguin	Royal African Co. had 47 servants in S.L.		
1722	Alliance of Dutch and Moors re-took Arguin from French			
1724	Royal African Co. took French forts at Albreda and Bintang. French once more expelled Dutch from Arguin			Dahomey pressed southwards, seeking access to the sea, and defeated opposing Oyo

Time Chart

DATE	SENEGAMBIA	SIERRA LEONE	GHANA	NIGERIA
1725	Royal African Co. lost 11 men in magazine explosion on James Fort			
1726		Royal African Co. abandoned York Fort because of Sherbro hostility		
1727		Temne allied with 8 Portuguese against British at Bunce		Oyo came to Ouidah's rescue and defeated Dahomey
1728		Royal African Co. abandoned Bunce Fort		Dahomey now paying tribute to Oyo
1729		Muslim Jihad started in Futa Jallon		
1730			[British Parliament began to give Royal African Co. grant to maintain forts	
1731				Gobir attacks on Kano began
1737				Oyo attacked Dahomey capital, Abomey
1738			Asante began to press against barrier of peoples between them and coast	

West Africa in History

DATE	SENEGAMBIA	SIERRA LEONE	GHANA	NIGERIA
1743				Gobir attacks on Kano ceased
			[*War of Spanish Succession began*	
1745		John Newton slave-dealing in Plantain Islands		
1747				Abomey defenders surrendered to Oyo who exacted heavy tribute
			[*Royal African Co. ceased to receive Parliamentary grant*	
1748				Gaha became Basorun of Oyo
			[*Peace of Aix-la-Chapelle*	
1749			[*'Regulated' Co. of Merchants Trading to Africa formed*	
1750			Kusi Obodum succeeded Opoku Ware as Asantehene	
1751			Anglican missionary Thomas Thompson now in Cape Coast	
1752			[*Royal African Co. dissolved*	
1756			[*Seven Years' War broke out*	
1757			French failed to capture Cape Coast castle	

Time Chart

DATE	SENEGAMBIA	SIERRA LEONE	GHANA	NIGERIA
1758	British captured French forts at Goree and Senegal, and burnt Albreda		British built Apollonia Fort in Nzima	
1760			Asante and Fante allied against Wassaw. Britain friendly with Asante	
1763	Albreda and Goree returned to France, Senegal to Britain		[*Peace of Paris*	
1764			Osei Kojo became Asantehene on death of Kusi Obodum	Gobir destroyed Zamfara's capital Birnin
1765	Senegambia became a Crown Province		Asante attacked Wassaw, Akim and Fante, and alienated British	Katsina helped Zamfarawa to rebuild his capital at Anka
1766	Governor O'Hara ruled Senegambia from St. Louis (Senegal)		First West African priest, Philip Quacoe, returned to G.C. from England	
1767			Britain now allying with Fante rather than Asante	
1768			Dutch tending to ally with Asante	

151

West Africa in History

DATE	SENEGAMBIA	SIERRA LEONE	GHANA	NIGERIA
1770		Liverpool firm abandoned factory on S.L. River whose agent was murdered		
1772			Asante again seeking access to coastal trade [*Mansfield's judgment freed slaves in Britain*	
1774			Committee of Company of London Merchants admitted need for bribery	
1776	Governor O'Hara left			
1777			Osei Kwame succeeded Osei Kojo as Asantehene	
1778	French captured St Louis Fort			
			[*War of American Independence*	
1779	French finally destroyed James Fort			
1780			British failed to take Dutch fort at Elmina	
1781			British failed again at Elmina, but took 6 other Dutch forts	

Time Chart

DATE	SENEGAMBIA	SIERRA LEONE	GHANA	NIGERIA
1782			Dutch captured British fort at Sekondi and destroyed it	Oyo power weakening because of weakness of Alafin
1783	Senegal recognized by Britain as French, Gambia by France as British		Dutch recaptured all forts lost in 1781 to British [*Peace of Versailles signed. African Association formed*]	
1784		French Govt. rented land from King Forbana.		
1785	Senegambia ceased to be a Crown Province	Liverpool firm re-opened factory on S.L. River		Dahomey ceased to pay tribute to Oyo
1786	Committee of Merchants administered forts in Gambia	London Co. leased Bunce to private slave trader who rebuilt it		
1787		First settlers arrived in Freetown to establish Province of Freedom		Alafin of Oyo, with help from his Kakanfo, regained control of his Basorun
1788		'Treaties' thumbprinted by Kings Tom and Naimbana		

West Africa in History

DATE	SENEGAMBIA	SIERRA LEONE	GHANA	NIGERIA
1789		Temne King Jimmy destroyed Province of Freedom		
1790	African Association's explorer Houghton teached Bambuk via Gambia	Private tenant of Bunce died		
1791		Sierra Leone Co. formed to re-found colony for commercial purposes	[Sierra Leone Company formed in London	
1792		Nova Scotians arrived in Freetown. John Clarkson first Governor	Danes at Christiansborg allied with Asante against British and Fante	
1793		French factory on King Forbana's land closed.	[Napoleonic Wars began	
1794		French expedition attacked S.L. from Goree		
1795			[Dutch East India Company liquidated	
1796		Vai had by now reached Gallinas		

Time Chart

DATE	SENEGAMBIA	SIERRA LEONE	GHANA	NIGERIA
1798		Mende had by now reached south of S.L.		
1799		.		Bornu by now cultural leader of the north

Printed in Great Britain
by Amazon

40050882R00098